Reasoning and Writing

A Direct Instruction Program

Level A
Teacher's Guide

Siegfried Engelmann

Karen Lou Seitz Davis

A Division of The McGraw·Hill Companies

Columbus, Ohio

Cover Credits

(tl, tr) PhotoDisc, (bl) Comstock.

SRA/McGraw-Hill

A Division of The McGraw·Hill Companies

Send all inquiries to:
SRA/McGraw-Hill
8787 Orion Place
Columbus, OH 43240-4027

Printed in the United States of America.

ISBN 0-02-684755-8

3 4 5 6 7 8 9 DBH 06 05 04 03

Contents

Program Summary

Facts about *Reasoning and Writing, Level A*

Children who are appropriately placed in Level A	Children who are in a beginning reading program and who have basic language-comprehension skills (children who pass placement test)
Placement criteria	A score of 5 or more on placement test (See page 17)
Format of lessons	Scripted presentations for all activities Program designed for presentation to entire class
Number of lessons	70 total (including 7 test lessons)
Scheduled time for Language periods	30–35 minutes per period for teacher-directed activities Additional 10–15 minutes for independent work
Weekly schedule	2, 3 or 5 periods per week. (Schedule depends on children's reading skills)
Teacher's material	Teacher's Guide Presentation Book
Children's material	Program material: 　　Workbook 1, Lessons 1–35 　　Workbook 2, Lessons 36–70 Additional materials: 　　crayon set that includes pink, purple and gray 　　　(or a pencil for gray) 　　scissors 　　pencil 　　paste 　　ruler
In-program tests	Lessons 10, 20, 30, 40, 50, 60, 70
Remedies	See page 79, Test Remedies
Additional material	*Writing Extensions, Level 1* 　　Teacher's Presentation and 　　　blackline masters for extension 　　　lessons 1–50

Scope and Sequence for *Reasoning and Writing, Level A*

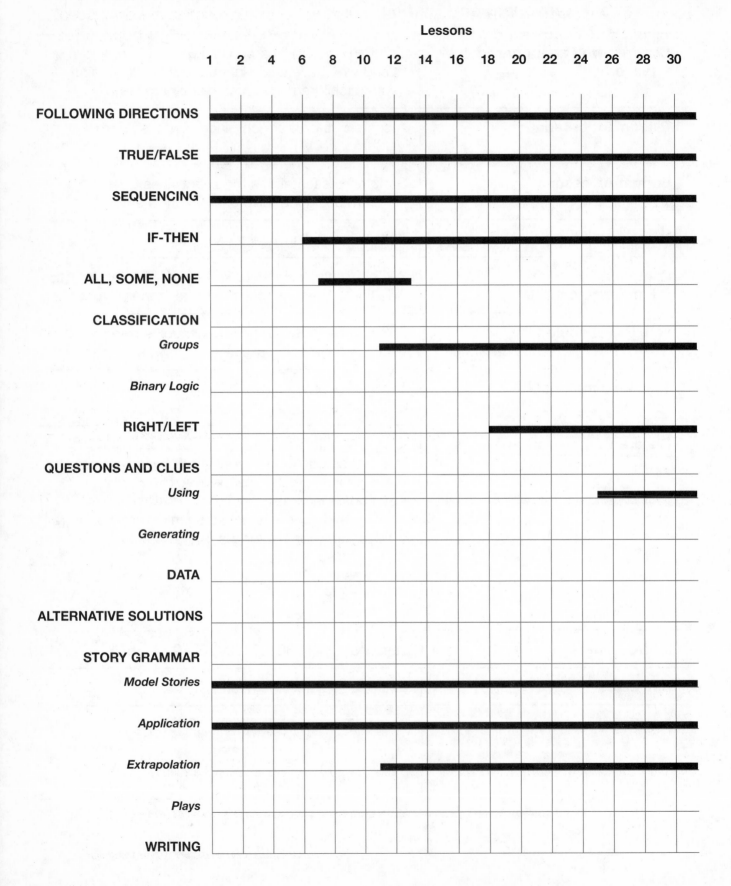

The Scope-and-Sequence chart shows the various tracks taught in Level A. Each track develops skills in a major topic, such as Sequencing or Classification. The **heavy** lines on the chart show the lessons on which the track begins and ends. The tracks and instructional approaches are discussed in the Tracks section of this book. (See page 30.)

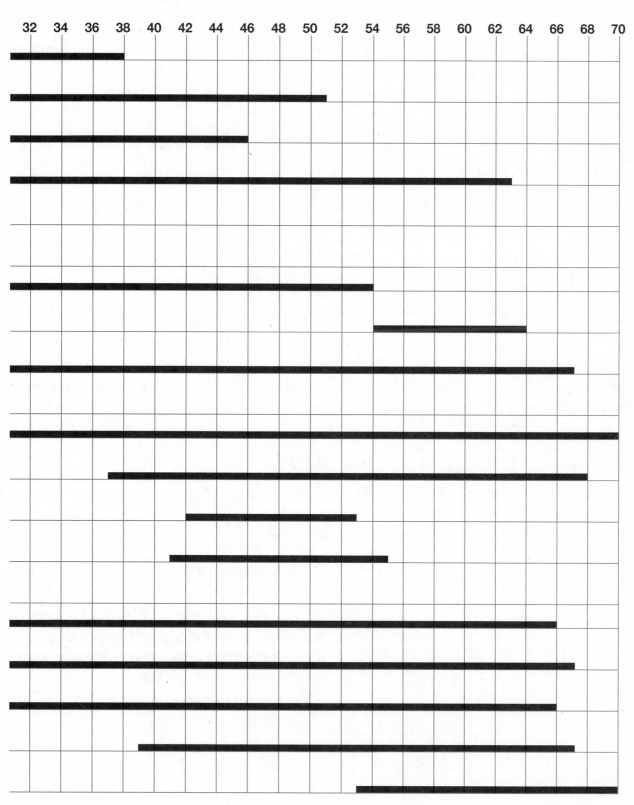

Scheduling

Reasoning and Writing A may be used in different ways, depending on the reading instruction that is being provided.

Here are four different plans for using Level A. The first two plans are for lower performers (disadvantaged children and others who score 5 or less on the placement test):

Plan 1	
Kindergarten	*Language for Learning* through Lesson 100
Grade 1	*Reasoning and Writing A*— 3 lessons per week

Plan 2	
Grade 1	*Language for Learning* through Lesson 100 *Reasoning and Writing A*— 5 lessons per week

Both plans provide for teaching *Reasoning and Writing* in grade 1. Plan 1 presents *Language for Learning* in kindergarten, ideally presented daily. Children should complete at least 100 lessons of the program and should master the material presented in these lessons before beginning *Reasoning and Writing. Reasoning and Writing* is presented in grade 1 on a 3-day-a-week schedule. This schedule assures that children's reading skills will be adequate for tasks involving reading presented in later lessons of Level A.

Plan 2 introduces *Language for Learning...* daily in first grade. After children complete 100

lessons (in about mid-February), they begin working on *Reasoning and Writing* 5 days a week.

Here's a plan for average performers (who pass the placement test):

Plan 3	
Grade 1	*Reasoning and Writing A*— 2 days per week or 3 days per week

The 2-day-a-week schedule is preferable if you don't plan to present intensive cooperative "authoring" during the latter part of grade 1. (See page 77.) If you plan cooperative authoring, the 3-day-a-week schedule is preferable because it allows approximately 30 lessons after the completion of Level A to work on "authoring."

Here's a plan for accelerated children. These are average or above-average performers who pass the placement test and who are relatively advanced in reading (reading on a beginning second-grade level by the middle of the first-grade year).

Plan 4	
Grade 1	*Reasoning and Writing A*— 5 days per week *Reasoning and Writing B*— 5 days per week

These children would complete Level B of *Reasoning and Writing* by the end of the first grade. They would be scheduled to go into Level C in the second grade. This schedule is reasonable for children who will be reading on the third-grade level during second grade.

How the Program Is Different

Reasoning and Writing teaches higher-order thinking skills, the kind that are needed for later reading, writing and thinking. The program differs from traditional approaches to teaching these comprehension skills in the following ways:

FIELD-TESTED

Reasoning and Writing has been shaped through extensive field testing and revising based on problems children and teachers encountered. This work was completed before the program was published. The development philosophy of *Reasoning and Writing* is that, if teachers or children have trouble with material presented, the program is at fault. Revisions are made to correct the problems.

ORGANIZATION

The organization of how skills are introduced, developed and reviewed is unique. In traditional programs, the curriculum is called a spiral, which means that children work exclusively on a particular topic for a few lessons. Then a new topic (often unrelated to the preceding topic) is presented. *Reasoning and Writing* does not follow this format for the following reasons:

a. During a period, it is not productive to work only on a single topic. If new information is being presented, it is very easy for children to become overwhelmed with the information. A more sensible procedure, and one that has been demonstrated to be superior in studies of learning and memory, is to distribute the practice so that, instead of working 30 minutes on a single topic, children work each day for possibly 7 minutes on each of four topics.

b. When full-period topics are presented, it becomes very difficult for the teacher to provide practice on the latest skills that had been taught. Unless the skills that had been taught are used and reviewed, children's performance will deteriorate, and the skills will have to be retaught when they again appear. A more sensible organization is to present work on skills continuously (not discontinuously), so that children work on a particular topic (such as true/false) for part of 20 or 30 lessons, not for 5 or 6 entire lessons at a time. In this context of continuous development of skills, review becomes automatic, and reteaching becomes unnecessary because children use the skills on almost every lesson.

c. When skills are not developed continuously, children must learn a lot of new concepts during a short period and are also expected to become "automatic" in applying the new concepts and skills. For most children, adequate learning will not occur. A better method is to develop skills and concepts in small steps so that children are not required to learn as much new material at a time. In this way they receive a sufficient amount of practice to become facile or automatic in applying what they learn.

d. When skills are not developed continuously, children and teachers may develop very negative attitudes about mastery. Children often learn that they are not expected to "learn" the new material because it will go away in a few days. Teachers become frustrated because they often understand that children need much more practice, but they are unable to provide it and at the same time move through the program at a reasonable rate. Again, the continuous development of skills solves this problem because children learn very quickly that what is presented is used, on this lesson, the next lesson and in many subsequent lessons. When the practice is sufficient, children develop the mindset or expectation needed for learning to mastery because the skill is something they will need in the immediate future.

e. When lessons are not clearly related to "periods" of time, the teacher has no precise way to gauge the performance of the children or to judge how long to spend on a particular "lesson." A more reasonable procedure is to organize material into lessons, each requiring so much time to teach. The teacher then knows that the lesson has the potential of teaching children within a class period of 30 minutes.

In *Reasoning and Writing,* skills are organized in *tracks.* A track is an ongoing development of a particular topic. Within each lesson, work from 3 to 5 tracks is presented. The teaching presentations are designed so it is possible to present the entire lesson in 30 minutes (although some lessons may run longer and some shorter, and more time may be needed for lower performers).

From lesson to lesson, the work on new skills develops a small step at a time so that children are not overwhelmed with new information and receive enough practice both to master skills and to become facile with them. Children, therefore, learn quickly about *learning new concepts* and realize that what they are learning has utility because they will use it.

HIGHER-ORDER THINKING SKILLS

***Reasoning and Writing* systematically teaches children to use higher-order thinking skills.** The program does not follow the current trends of merely exposing children to activities and assuming that they will learn something about reasoning or writing. The "exposure" approach is rejected in favor of systematic instruction for the following reasons:

a. Direct Instruction works best for teaching comprehension skills.

b. Later activities are more manageable if children have been taught the various component skills needed to engage meaningfully in the activities. When children are taught component skills, the teacher knows what the children have learned and can more easily correct mistakes. The correction does not involve extensive teaching during work on later activities, but merely reminds children of what they have already learned.

c. When all children are prepared for an elaborate activity, **all**—not some—can be expected to perform perfectly or near perfectly. The activity will not discriminate against lower performers, who often learn very little from an activity if they are simply exposed to it. The reason is that they don't have the background knowledge needed to approach the activity sensibly. It would require far too much time to identify the various skills and knowledge they lack and teach them before proceeding in the activity.

PREPARATION FOR READING AND WRITING

The higher-order thinking skills presented in *Reasoning and Writing A* are designed to prepare children for later work in both reading and writing (grades 2 and above).

a. **Story Grammar.** When children read, they are expected to get a sense of the story so they can anticipate what will happen and can relate events that occur to what they know about the characters or the situations presented. To prepare students for this type of understanding, Level A teaches children about story grammar.

b. **Sequencing.** When children relate what they read to an illustration of the story, they are expected to understand which part of the story is illustrated and how particular details of the picture correspond to details of the story. These relationships involve an understanding of sequencing.

   The illustration is static, although it portrays action. The details of a picture would "change" if it illustrated the event that occurred next in the story. Level A teaches the perspective necessary for children to relate details to sequences.

c. **Classification.** When children write in grades 3 and 4, they are expected to describe events and scenes. Much of what they are to describe presumes knowledge of classification, not merely the classification of objects, but also of events. **Four people were *busy* in the yard.** The people were doing different things; however, all were the same in that they were **busy.** Another example: **Four buildings were near the farmhouse.** The constructions are from different subclasses (barn, shed, garage and workshop), but they all are in the class of buildings.

   Level A teaches classification that is relevant to the functional use of class words in writing and in expressing ideas clearly.

d. **Reasoning.** Much of what children are expected to understand when they read, and express when they write, has to do with "reasons." One type of reasoning can be expressed through if-then statements. **If it rains, Susan won't go to the park.** Some reasoning involves "elimination" strategies. **The ball is not inside the house. So it must be outside the house.** A variation of the elimination strategy is used with "clues." If you know that you're trying to find a vehicle that has four wheels, you can eliminate boats, trains, large trucks, bikes, trikes, motorcycles and other vehicles that do not have four wheels.

   Level A introduces children to a broad range of reasoning activities. They learn to apply if-then rules. They follow directions that have the words **all, some** and **none.** They use clues to eliminate possibilities and identify the only possibility that hasn't been eliminated, and they deal with "problems" that can be solved by applying "binary reasoning"; for example, **She moved the teeter-totter so the right end is down. She didn't touch the right end. So she must have pushed up on the left end.**

APPLICATION

All the instruction in *Reasoning and Writing A* points toward actual applications, not merely to answering questions. Activities are designed so children actually **do** things to create changes. Furthermore, these activities are designed so that it is easy for the teacher to judge whether children approached the application appropriately.

a. The major thrust of the sequencing instruction involves activities in which children either use symbols to create a sequence of events or refer to symbols to reconstruct a series of events. An example of the first type of sequencing involves a static picture that shows a character in a scene.

Here's one of the simpler activities from Level A.

Although the picture shows the character in one position, the teacher tells the various things the character did—backed up, ran to the bank of the stream, landed on the rock and then fell into the stream. The numbers show where she did these things. Children recount the series of events by telling what happened first (circle 1), next (circle 2) and so forth. This type of activity provides children with the perspective of looking at a static picture and relating it to earlier and later events.

Another variation is the activity in which children listen to a sequence of events; write the appropriate numbers for what happens first, next and so forth; then refer to the sequence of numbers and retell the story. For both activities, the emphasis is directly on children creating or reproducing the sequence of events, not merely answering questions about "which happened first."

b. Similarly, various reasoning activities require children to create changes that bring about specific outcomes. For instance, children are presented a picture such as this one.

Children describe the apples: **Some of the apples have a leaf.** We want the picture to show something different. Possibly, we want the picture to show **none of the apples have a leaf** (which can be achieved by crossing out the apples that have a leaf). Possibly, we want *all of the apples to have a leaf* (which involves drawing leaves on some of the apples or crossing out apples that don't have a leaf). Children change the picture so it is consistent with the desired outcome. Although they answer true/false questions about the picture before and after they change it, the primary focus of the activity is on the change and the logic of the change. "Before you changed the picture, all of the apples had a leaf. True or false? After you changed the picture, all of the apples had a leaf. True or false?"

Children also do a lot of work with classes. The activities are "clue games," in which the children refer to objects in a class. The teacher gives a clue. Based on the clue, children turn over the pictures the clue **eliminates.** For instance, if they have pictures of vehicles and the teacher indicates that **the mystery vehicle has two wheels,** children turn over the pictures that could not be the mystery vehicle. The activity teaches children fundamental properties of classes. As they receive more information through additional clues, they turn over more and more vehicles. As they do this, they are making the class of possibilities smaller and the class of eliminated members larger, until there is only one possibility left. The questions the teacher asks focus on the information provided by the various clues. "How did you know that the mystery vehicle wasn't a bicycle? It has two wheels." Answer: *Because one clue said that it had a motor, and a bicycle doesn't have a motor.*

c. Level A presents activities in which children complete and construct displays that show if-then possibilities, such as, *If it snows, Clarabelle will go skiing.*

Other activities involve working within systems that are "binary" in structure. For instance, children work with two-rung ladders:

They fix up the ladder to show specific outcomes. "Listen: Fix up the ladder so the bottom rung is longer than the top rung, but don't do anything to the bottom rung . . . ." (Children erase part of the top rung.)

d. The writing that children do in Level A also follows the construction format. Children are provided with various pictures and words that can be used to construct different sentences.

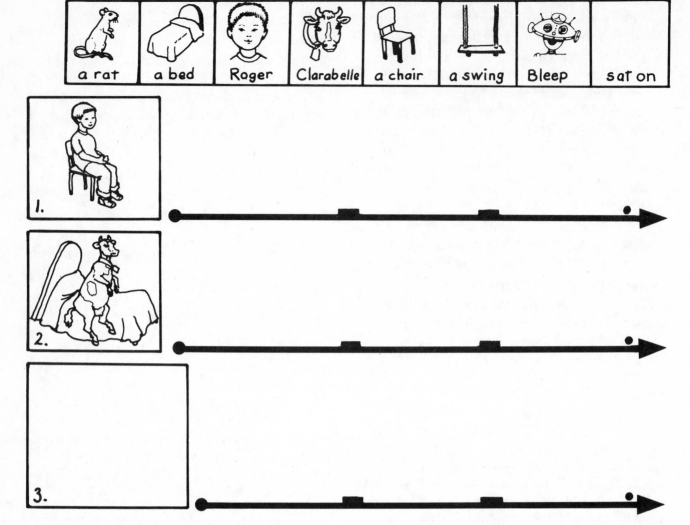

Children select the words for their sentences and write them. Note that it is possible to make up some pretty "silly" sentences with the words; however, the structure of the sentences will not be silly. All sentences are based on the idea that writing and grammar begin with sentences that start with the subject and end with the predicate. In Level C of *Reasoning and Writing,* children will build upon this idea to construct a variety of sentences based on the subject-predicate order. (First you name; then you tell what that person or thing did.)

The work in Level A introduces children to the idea that words can be used to express ideas that are fun, and that the sentences express something that can be "illustrated." (For many activities, children draw a picture of the sentence they create.) This introduction to writing also acquaints children with one of the ultimate constraints of writing, which is that the individual words must be spelled and capitalized appropriately. (For much work, spelling approximations are permissible; however, for writing in a context that presents the words and shows how they are spelled, misspelling is not permitted.)

In all these activities, children produce changes that provide the teacher with strong evidence about what the children are learning and about specific conceptual problems they may be experiencing. This structure makes correcting specific mistakes manageable and, at the same time, assures that children are applying what they have learned.

STORIES

Reasoning and Writing A has been designed like a well-constructed reading program, except that it focuses on the comprehension skills, not the reading. In other respects, however, it parallels a good reading program. The reading program introduces various "skills," primarily decoding skills, and then presents stories that incorporate these skills. As children learn more skills, the stories become more central to the learning. After the beginning levels, the stories drive the instruction.

Reasoning and Writing follows this procedure. The central focus of each lesson is the story. The story typically comes at the end of the lesson. For the children, it's the payoff—the dessert. It is also the vehicle that both integrates what children learn and teaches them about the structure of stories. While it teaches "story grammar," the teaching focus is like that of the other activities in Level A—on construction. Children learn about stories in such a way that they can construct stories according to the constraints of different story grammars.

The stories are uniquely designed for this teaching, and the sequence of stories is designed to assure that all children learn important higher-order skills associated with stories. This knowledge sets the stage for comprehension work that the children will do later in their reading program. The stories in Level A specifically address those aspects of comprehension that typically give older students trouble when reading stories.

Story Grammar

Researchers have documented that entertaining stories follow a kind of "grammar." A story presents a character who has a problem. The details of the story and information about the character suggest possible solutions to the problem. They also suggest an outcome—such as bad guys fail to solve the problem; good guys and underdogs succeed.

Facts and research about story grammar do not imply what children should be taught or why. There may be some advantage in requiring children to **identify** the character, the setting, the problem, the instrumental activity the character engages in to solve the problem, and the outcome. The primary problem with this approach is that it provides children with relatively sterile information and, in some cases, requires them to write summaries that involve very sophisticated summary skills. *A Christmas Carol,* for instance, tells about Scrooge and his encounters with specters that challenge his values and outlook. Although it is possible to write a summary of the problems Scrooge encountered, the summary would be very sterile and difficult to write and would provide a very poor test of somebody's understanding of story grammar. A far better test of understanding would be for a person to predict the outcome of the story or (better yet) create a parallel story based on the same structure as *A Christmas Carol.*

Level A teaches children how to create parallel stories based on familiar story grammars. For this teaching, model stories are introduced. Each model has a unique story grammar. Through later activities, children extrapolate the details of the model stories to create new stories with the same grammar.

PAUL

Paul has predictable behaviors:

He loves to paint—but in only two colors, pink and purple.

Paul speaks in p-starting words: "Purple plums would be perfectly pleasing."

He has a predictable solution to problems of spilled paint. If paint plops onto the porch while Paul is painting a pretty picture of purple plums, Paul says something like, "That porch looks poor with puddles of purple paint on it, but I can fix it." His solution: Paint the whole porch purple.

In the first story, purple paint gets on the pane of a window, the porch and other places. Paul solves each problem. Then his brother comes out and gets paint on his pants. His pants are a mess, but Paul says, "But brother, don't worry. I can fix it." The story doesn't tell how he does that, but the children know because the story grammar is very strong.

The children hear the model story about Paul in three different lessons. Later in the program, they use their knowledge of Paul to extrapolate. They identify unique utterances that Paul would make; they compose utterances (with p-starting words); they compose endings to new stories involving Paul and they make up entire stories.

SWEETIE

The second character introduced is a nasty cat named Sweetie, whose story grammar is completely different from Paul's. Sweetie's grammar is quite sophisticated because it always involves misunderstandings that are based on perspective.

Sweetie loves to chase things like little birds or helpless butterflies. His plans center around getting something to eat, and he says things like, "Yum, yum. I'll just go over there and grab a pawful of little brown birds."

Sweetie is always foiled because he lacks information about what really takes place when he tries to execute his plan. Sweetie always thinks that he was foiled by his helpless prey and says something like, "From here those birds look pretty helpless, but let me tell you, they are big and strong."

In the first Sweetie story, Bonnie puts up a large birdbath in the yard next door. Sweetie sees all the little birds that are attracted to the birdbath and says, "Yum, yum. Look at all those little birds. I'm going to sneak over to that birdbath. . . ." So he sneaks through a hole in the fence and moves slowly through the bushes until the birdbath is within leaping range. Just then, Sweetie hears a terrible squabble in the birdbath, but he can't see what's happening. An eagle decided to take a bath, and when that eagle swooped down, all the other birds took off. Sweetie, still thinking that the little birds are in the birdbath, leaps up to grab a pawful of birds, but that eagle grabs Sweetie and slams him into the birdbath. Splash! Sweetie darts across the yard and through the hole in the fence. Finally, he peeks back at the birdbath, but in the meantime the eagle has finished its bath and taken off. The other birds have returned. Sweetie looks at them and says to himself, "From here, those birds look pretty small and helpless. But when you get close to them, they are really big and strong. I don't think I'll go near that birdbath again."

Again, the grammar is generalizable to other situations, which are presented after children have heard the model story three times. Children predict how the new stories will end, what Sweetie will say, what he thinks happened versus what actually happened. They also can identify unique utterances that Sweetie (versus Paul) might make: "Yum, yum, those are tasty looking butterflies . . . ."

As with the Paul stories, the children demonstrate their knowledge of the grammar not by merely identifying characters or problems, but by creating outcomes that are consistent with the story grammar.

THE BRAGGING RATS

The next main story is about two rats who constantly argue about who is best at doing something. When describing how good they are, they go beyond exaggeration to incredible lies. After it becomes apparent to all the rats that the Bragging Rats do not know how to settle their argument, the wise old rat intervenes and shows them how to stage a contest to determine which Bragging Rat is the best. Other rats, one of whom is the little black rat, are permitted to engage in these contests. The outcome is always the same. The little black rat finishes first, and the Bragging Rats perform poorly. At the end of each story, the Bragging Rats find something else to argue about, and the other rats leave in disgust.

In the first Bragging Rats story, the rats argue about who is the fastest runner. The wise old rat sets up a course that goes to the edge of the pond and then back to the starting line. The two Bragging Rats get tangled up just before they turn around, tumble into the pond and don't finish the race. The little black rat wins. But the contest is for naught because the Bragging Rats are now arguing about who is the fastest swimmer. "I may not be the fastest **runner** in this bunch, but there is no rat in the world that can **swim** as fast as I can."

The story grammar is extrapolated to different stories and to a play about which Bragging Rat is the strongest.

CLARABELLE

Clarabelle is a cow whose story grammar is greatly different from that of Paul or Sweetie or the Bragging Rats. Clarabelle loves to imitate other animals and even people. Her plans always fail for the same reason: She's very heavy. As the first Clarabelle story says, "When she jumped into the duck pond, all the water jumped out of the pond."

The predictable aspects of the grammar are:

* Clarabelle will try to do something that somebody else does.
* Because of her weight, she fails.
* The outcome is humorous.
* The people or animals she tries to imitate become annoyed with her.

In the first Clarabelle story, Clarabelle observes a group of bluebirds sitting on a wire attached near the hayloft of the barn. Clarabelle decides that she wants to sit on that wire with the birds. Some of the other farm animals try to warn her not to do it and remind her of some of her past fiascoes, but Clarabelle climbs up to the loft and tiptoes out onto the wire. The wire sags down under her weight, and the bluebirds are not at all happy. "This wire is for bluebirds, not brown-and-white cows."

Finally, Clarabelle decides to get off the wire. Going back into the loft would require going uphill, and Clarabelle is just above a mound of hay, so she decides to jump down from the wire. When she does, the wire springs up and shoots the bluebirds into the clouds, leaving blue feathers fluttering here and there. Naturally, the other farm animals roll around in laughter, but Clarabelle is not at all happy.

In a later parallel story, Clarabelle decides to imitate the school children who line up and get on the school bus. The bus stands up on end when she moves to the back of it.

Another Clarabelle story has Clarabelle fascinated with the idea of going off a diving board and into a swimming pool. When she does, the board breaks and everybody gets mad at Clarabelle.

ROLLA

Rolla's story grammar presents another type of "perspective" confusion. Rolla is a merry-go-round horse who wears the number 8. That number bothers her because there are only eight horses, and she's number 8. So one day she executes her plan to change her number. She thinks that if she could go faster, she could pass up the horse in front of her, and then she'd be number 7. Or better yet, she could pass up all the other horses and be number 1.

When she attempts to go faster, the other horses go faster, the music speeds up and sounds awful, and the merry-go-round goes so fast that nobody will go on it. As one mother puts it, "This is like a rodeo." Rolla becomes depressed when she realizes that her plan won't work, and the other horses are concerned because they're exhausted from streaking around in circles. They ask Rolla questions and discover her problem. They solve it by giving Rolla the number 1. Everybody is happy.

In a later story, Rolla feels that she is too close to number 8, the horse right in front of her. To create a greater distance between herself and number 8 she . . . . The children make up an ending to show how the other horses ensure that Rolla can't see horse number 8.

BLEEP

Bleep is an imperfect robot invented by Molly Mixup, whose nickname comes from the fact that none of her inventions work exactly the way they should. Although Bleep is very talented, he has some unusual personality characteristics:

He always says "bleep" at the beginning of his sentences.

He often replies to directions such as, "Get the paint from the garage," by saying, "Bleep. Okay, baby."

His verbal reports are sometimes unreliable (or confusing).

The Bleep story grammar is more complicated than those of the other characters because it is developed over a sequence of stories. The first sequence is a three-episode story in which Bleep incorrectly relays a phone message. He has a phone conversation with a friend of Molly's, Mrs. Anderson, who thinks she is talking to Molly, not Bleep. Mrs. Anderson asks if "Molly" has a preference about where the two women will meet for lunch. Bleep indicates that there is a wonderful restaurant at the corner of 13th and Elm; however, the only thing on that corner is a wrecking yard. The women arrive at different times (Molly in a red van and Mrs. Anderson in a red sports car), park their cars in front of the wrecking yard (in drop-off zones) and search for the restaurant. They run into each other and return to their respective cars, only to find that the cars have been dismantled and that the workers are ready to scrunch the remains of each vehicle. Molly gives the workers directions for reassembling the vehicles, but the results are two red vehicles—each half-sports-car and half-van. Nobody is very happy.

The Bleep story grammar is extended in later stories that involve Molly adjusting the screws in Bleep's head. Each adjustment results in unexpected changes in the way Bleep talks or in the things he remembers. In later stories, Molly must reteach Bleep the days of the week and the months of the year because he has somehow lost memory of them and replaced them with "blurp" words. So in saying the days of the week, Bleep would say, "Sunday, Monday, Tuesday, Blurpday, Blurpday . . . ."

OTHER STORIES

Other story sequences in the program follow the format of having unique story grammars. The characters include Roger (who loves hats but always has problems with them), Roxie (who collects rocks) and Andrea (a shy little mouse who is friends with a dog named Honey, but who hates Sweetie).

SUMMARY

Here are important points about the story-grammar-activities presented in Level A.

1. The grammars prepare children for comprehension activities in many of the stories they will read. Well-written stories present characters that have distinguishing features, that reason and dream, that do things to reach goals. These stories present problems or conflicts and outcomes that are largely implied by the story details. Children who have learned the various grammars presented in Level A have a working understanding of a full range of story grammars. This working knowledge helps children focus their attention on details of stories they read, make predictions that are implied by the details of stories and characters, and engage more actively in stories than children who are less sophisticated in story construction.

2. The grammars prepare children for writing activities. Although extensive story writing does not begin until Level C, the early work on grammars provides children with the basic knowledge they need to be constructors of interesting stories, not merely critics or categorizers of story details. By the end of Level A, they will have engaged in many "construction" activities (participating in plays, making up oral stories) that require applying knowledge of the various grammars.

3. Many story-grammars presented in Level A are not the type that can be easily summarized in terms of setting, character, problem and so forth. The reason is that each grammar presents characters who have a unique way of thinking and behaving. Consider the Bragging Rats. What is their "problem"? Part of their problem is their "personalities," their ineffective way of settling arguments and their undaunted tendencies to ignore data and to lie. Part of their problem is the particular situation associated with their argument.

   Knowledge of the "Bragging Rat format" goes far beyond simple summaries or labels of plot and character. That the children are able to perform on extensive extrapolation activities by the end of Level A provides evidence that they have learned much more about story grammar than what is typically taught to children who are much older than they are.

4. The stories serve as the main avenue for the instruction that is provided in Level A. Skills are taught in different tracks; however, all skills are related to stories. Sometimes a new skill will be introduced first in a story (such as naming days of the week, which appears first in a Bleep story and then is further developed in the Writing track). Other skills are introduced through instruction that is not related to the stories or story characters, but these skills later appear in the stories. For example, right and left are introduced in the Right/Left track. The concepts are then incorporated in story-grammar activities. For example, a later Bragging Rats story revolves around an argument about how to get out of a maze. One rat says that he got out by making only right turns. The other rat disagrees. The wise old rat settles the argument. To discover which rat is correct, the children test alternative routes on an illustration of the maze.

Similarly, true/false, classification, binary logic, if-then reasoning, data collection and all the other skills taught in the program are called for in different story-grammar applications.

5. Perhaps most important, the children "love" the stories. Part of the reason has to do with the characters. They are not necessarily wonderful, sharing individuals who do everything that is sweet and wholesome. Instead, they get in trouble and make mistakes—two qualities that the children readily identify with.

The stories are the last part of the lessons. They serve as a motivator for the other lesson activities. Although children generally treat them as dessert, the stories are very powerful vehicles for teaching skills that are both sophisticated and useful.

Placement Testing

Level A is appropriate for all children who have basic language skills and who are placed in a beginning-reading program. (If children are not placed in a reading program, they will have trouble with those items presented near the end of the program that presuppose beginning-reading skills.)

The placement test evaluates children's abilities to follow directions and to use knowledge of prepositions (which is a good indicator of basic language skills).

A reproducible copy of the placement test appears on page 18. The test is group administered and requires about 10 minutes for children to complete. The script for presenting the test appears below.

Administering the Test

Pass out a test form to each child.

Children are to write their name in the space on top. (Make sure you can identify each test.)

Present the following 3 non-scorable (warm-up) items and 4 scorable items.

> "I'm going to tell you to do some very hard things. See if you can do them."

Note: These are non-scorable items.

- "Touch a picture that has a cup in it. A cup."
  (Observe children and give feedback.)
- "Touch a picture that has a pencil in it. A pencil."
  (Observe children and give feedback.)
- "Touch a picture that has a book in it. A book."
  (Observe children and give feedback.)

Note: These are scorable items.

"Now come the really tough items."

Item 1. "One of the pictures shows the pencil under the book. The pencil **under** the book. Find that picture." (Pause.) "Draw a circle around that picture. Circle the picture that shows the pencil **under** the book. Raise your hand when you're finished."

Note: When presenting item 1, make sure that children are attending to and attempting to follow the directions. If some children seem lost, tell them, "Touch the picture that shows the pencil under the book." Don't tell them whether their response is correct or not, but after they have touched a picture, say, "Circle that picture." Do not prompt for the remaining items.

Item 2. "One of the pictures shows the pencil **over** the book. The pencil over the book. Find that picture." (Pause.) "Listen: Make a line right through that picture. Make a line through the picture that shows the pencil **over** the book. Raise your hand when you're finished."

Item 3. "One of the pictures shows the pencil **next to** the book. The pencil next to the book. Find that picture." (Pause.) "Make a big dot in the middle of that picture. Make a big dot in the middle of the picture that shows the pencil **next to** the book. Raise your hand when you're finished."

Item 4. "One of the pictures shows the pencil **on** the book. The pencil on the book. Find that picture." (Pause.) "Write your first name on that picture. Write your name on the picture that shows the pencil **on** the book. Raise your hand when you're finished."

Scoring the Test

An answer key appears on page 19. The test consists of 4 scorable items. Each item is worth 2 points. One point is awarded if the child has put some kind of mark on a correct item. A second point is awarded if the item is marked correctly.

- A perfect score is 8.
- Add the points for the correct pictures: 3, 5, 7 and 11. Award 1 point for each of these pictures if there's a mark of some sort in it. Award a second point for each picture (3, 5, 7 and 11) that has the **right** mark. Give children the benefit of the doubt. If they don't circle the whole picture but part of it, give them credit for performing correctly; if they reasonably approximate the markings called for by the other instructions, give them credit.

Subtract 2 points for any picture that is marked other than pictures 3, 5, 7 and 11.

Placement Criteria

Children pass the test if they achieve a score of 5 or more. If 80% of the children pass the test, *Reasoning and Writing* is appropriate to present to the entire class.

Special work will be needed with those children who do not pass the test. The recommendation for these children is placement in *Language for Learning* (especially children with a score of 3 or less). See page 4 for more details.

Placement Test

Name: _____

1.	**2.**	**3.**
4.	**5.**	**6.**
7.	**8.**	**9.**
10.	**11.**	**12.**

Reasoning and Writing, Level A

Placement
Test

Name: _____

1.	2.	3.
4.	5.	6.
7.	8.	9.
10.	11. child's name	12.

Teaching the Program

Level A is designed to be presented to the entire class. You should generally be able to teach one lesson during a 30–35 minute period. Children's independent work requires another 10–15 minutes. The independent work can be scheduled at another time during the day.

Organization

The program will run far more smoothly if you follow these steps:

* Arrange seating so you can receive very quick information on high performers and low performers. A good plan is to organize the children something like this:

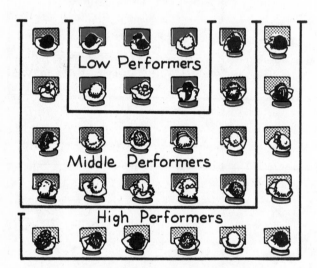

Front of Classroom

The lowest performers are closest to the front of the classroom. Middle performers are arranged around the lowest performers. Highest performers are arranged around the periphery. With this arrangement, you can position yourself so that, by taking a few steps during the time that children are working problems, you can sample low, average and high performers.

While different variations of this arrangement are possible, be careful not to seat low performers far from the front-center of the room. The highest performers, understandably, can be farthest from the center because they attend better, learn faster and need less observation and feedback.

* Arrange 4 permanent teams of children to work together in the team games. The grouping should be based on performance. Each team should have low performers, average performers and high performers.

Teaching

When you teach the program, a basic rule is that you shouldn't present from the front of the room unless you're showing something on the board.

For most of the activities, you direct children to work specified tasks. For these activities, you should present from somewhere in the middle of the room (in no set place); and, as children work the task, you should move around and quickly observe a good sample of children. Although you won't be able to observe every child working every task, you can observe at least half a dozen children in possibly 15 seconds.

Rehearse the lesson before presenting it to the class. Don't simply read the text—act it out.

Watch your wording. If you rehearse each of the early lessons before presenting them, you'll soon learn how to present efficiently from the script. In later lessons, you should scan the list of skills at the beginning of each lesson. New skills are in boldface type. If a new skill is introduced in a lesson, rehearse it. Most activities in the lesson will not be new, but will be a variation of what you've presented earlier, so you may not need to rehearse these activities.

Managing Activities

Because the emphasis of Level A is on "constructing" outcomes, children do a lot of marking and coloring. They also do some cutting and pasting. Procedures for organizing material so they are available for use in the lesson becomes an important issue in presenting Level A.

For every lesson, each child needs a set of crayons that contains pink, purple and gray. (If gray crayons are not available, direct students to use their pencil to make the gray marks or to shade things that should be gray.) Each child also needs a pencil.

Some lessons require children to have scissors and paste. Children often lack facility in working quickly with crayons, scissors and paste. A good management system reinforces them for working faster and more accurately.

Here are general procedures for shaping good work with materials.

1. Make sure that each child has the material needed for the lesson. One plan is to announce at the beginning of the lesson that it's time for the language lesson. Introduce the rule that you'll count to ten. All children who have their pencil and crayons on their desk and in place by the time you finish counting receive a good-work point (or sticker).

2. Establish the rule that children are not to play with their crayons or pencil until you tell them to use them. "Remember, don't play with your material." The simplest way to shape their behavior is to praise children who are working "big." "Wow, we have a lot of big people in this room. Everybody has their pencil and crayons in place and nobody is playing with them. Nice job." If playing with material becomes a problem, award bonus points (or stickers) for not playing with the material.

3. When pencils or crayons are used for activities that precede the story, establish rules for what children are to do with their material when they complete the activity. "Remember, when you're finished, crayons back in the box. Pencils back in place." Again, praise children who follow these rules. "I can tell a lot of people are already finished because I see a lot of desks with the material in its place. Good work."

After the structured lesson has been completed, children color the story picture and possibly other parts of the worksheet. This activity does not have to be scheduled as part of the lesson, but can be presented during "seat work" time.

4. Demonstrate procedures that require mechanical skills. Some children often have trouble coloring or shading an object. Often they "ballpark" it and go outside the boundary. The simplest way to shape this behavior is to tell the child: "You want to see somebody who knows how to do a super job? Watch me." Quickly color an object. "Look at that. I didn't have one mark that went outside that yellow cat. See if you can do that. No marks outside the thing you're coloring." Observe the child later and give feedback on improvements. "You're doing a lot better—only a couple of little marks outside the cat. That's almost perfect."

With repeated feedback (based on the idea that the child will not perform perfectly for a while, but will tend to improve), skills are shaped quickly. Children receive a lot of practice in Level A.

5. In lessons that require cutting, make sure that children have scissors (and possibly paste). In some lessons, children cut "flaps" on the margin of their workbook page and fold the flaps over. In other lessons, they cut out elements and paste them on a specified part of the page. The element to be cut out is always positioned at an outer edge of the page so that children are required to cut only three sides of the element, which is always in a dotted box.

(**Note:** In many lessons, children cut out elements and put them where they belong in the picture, but the script makes no reference to pasting the elements in place. You may assign the pasting as part of the "independent" work that follows the structured lesson. At that time, children also color pictures.)

6. Show children how to fold flaps over. For many games, children cut flaps along the margin, and then "fold over" specific pictures that "could not be the mystery object." Here's an example of a worksheet with "flaps."

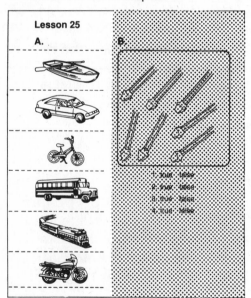

Children cut along the dotted lines that separate the pictures on the outside of the page. As the teacher gives clues about the mystery object, children fold over the pictures that could not be the mystery object.

Children often have trouble folding the flap so it's folded and stays down. Possibly the simplest procedure is to use a ruler.

- Grab a flap and pull it toward the center of the page as far as it will go without tearing.
- Place a ruler over the flap and press down hard.
- If you use this procedure, demonstrate how to do it. Make sure that each child has a ruler.

Another possible way to do it is to have children fold the flap under the page. This procedure is more mechanically involved, because when children fold over a later flap, some of the earlier-folded flaps may pop out. If you use this procedure, make sure that children use a ruler and press down hard after each new folding.

7. Many lessons require children to "draw" elements or make letters in the picture. The simplest way to shape this type of activity is to post children's material where all can see it. A good plan is to have two or three sections:

Super Stars   Stars   Emerging Stars

Post the best examples under Super Stars. Place work that shows improvement under Emerging Stars.

- When you first post material, make it clear that children will improve. "These are the Super Stars at drawing and coloring . . . . These are the Emerging Stars. We'll see what happens later. I'll bet that some of the Emerging Stars will end up being Super Stars before very long."

- When children move from one category to the next, make a fuss about it. "I want to call your attention to a new worksheet in the Super Star category. James has been an Emerging Star for a while and look what happened. His last worksheet is a Super Star. Good work, James."

A workable plan is to select one worksheet per week for display. Each child's worksheet is posted and remains posted for the week. If you follow this plan, remind the children, "Remember, today is the day when your work gets put on display, so try to do a super job."

- Try to use reasonable criteria for classifying the works. Tell children specifically what they have to do to reach a higher class. "If you just write your letters a little more carefully, you'll be a Star."

8. Present extension activities that give children an opportunity to use what they've learned in *Reasoning and Writing*. If the program is presented three times a week, children will complete the program after about 115 school days. To complete the school year, approximately 32 more lessons are needed. The last lesson in the program (lesson 70) introduces a writing format that involves the children (working in teams) in cooperatively developing stories based on the characters introduced in Level A. This type of activity can be used productively for the remainder of the year. Children can work out details of the story through their group. They present their ideas to you. If an idea is acceptable, you write it in the story. Later, they illustrate the story.

The biggest single management problem associated with this format is to make sure that each child is participating and understands the details of the proposed story. So when you consult with a group about a proposed story, call on different children to tell the whole story, before you write it. If some children are hazy on details, tell the group, "You're going to have to work harder on your plan. Before you call me back to hear your plan, make sure everybody knows the story and can tell the things that happen."

Provide additional suggestions based on the parts that were hazy or inconsistent.

Unless you place a strong individual-performance criterion on the work, some children will not be significantly involved and will not benefit much from the group work.

Using the Teacher Presentation Scripts

The script for each lesson indicates precisely how to present each structured activity. The script shows what you say, what you do, and what the children's responses should be.

What you say appears in blue type:
> You say this.

What you do appears in parentheses:
> (You do this.)

The responses of the children are in italics:
> *Children say this.*

Follow the specified wording in the script. While wording variations from the specified script are not always dangerous, you will be assured of communicating clearly with the children if you follow the script exactly. The reason is that the wording is controlled, and the tasks are arranged so they provide succinct wording and focus clearly on important aspects of what the children are to do. Although you may at first feel uncomfortable "reading" from a script (and you may feel that the children will not pay attention), follow the scripts very closely; try to present them as if you were saying something important to the children. If you do, you'll find after awhile that working from a script is not difficult and that children indeed respond well to what you say.

A sample script appears on page 25.

The arrows show the four different things you'll do that are not spelled out in the script. You'll make sure that group responses involve all the children. For some exercises, you'll write things on the board. You'll also "firm" critical parts of the exercises. And you'll use information based on what the children are doing to judge whether you'll proceed quickly or wait a few more seconds before moving on with the presentation.

ARROW 1: GROUP RESPONSES

Some of the tasks call for group responses. If children respond together in unison, you receive good information about whether "most" of the children are performing correctly. The simplest way to signal children to respond together is to adopt a timing practice—just like the timing in a musical piece.

Step 5 presents a task that children respond to in unison.

Everybody, say that sentence. (Signal.)
Paul painted a pot.

You can signal when children are to respond by nodding, clapping one time, snapping your fingers or tapping your foot. After initially establishing the timing for signals, you can signal through voice inflection only.

Children will not be able to initiate responses together at the appropriate rate unless you follow these rules.

a. Talk first. Pause a standard length of time (possibly 1 second); then signal. Children are to respond on your signal— not after it or before it.
b. Model responses that are paced reasonably. Don't permit children to produce slow, drony responses. These are dangerous because they rob you of

the information that can be derived from appropriate group responses. When children respond in a drony way, many of them are copying responses of others. If children are required to respond at a reasonable speaking rate, all children must initiate responses; therefore, it's relatively easy to determine which children are not responding and which are saying the wrong thing.

Also, don't permit children to respond at a very fast rate or to "jump" your signal.

To correct mistakes, show children exactly what you want them to do.

I'm good at saying it the right way. My turn to say that sentence: **Paul painted a pot.** Wasn't that great? Let's see who can do it just that way:
Everybody, say that sentence. (Signal.)
Paul painted a pot.
Good saying it the right way.

(**Note:** Do not respond with the children unless you are trying to work with them on a difficult response. You present only what's in blue. You do not say the answers with the children, and you should not move your lips or give other spurious clues about what the answer is.)

Think of unison responses this way: If you use them correctly, they provide you with much diagnostic information. They suggest whether you should repeat a task (because the response was weak). They permit you to get information about which children may need more help. They are therefore important early in the program. After children have learned the game, the children will be able to respond on cue with no signal. That will happen, however, only if you always keep a constant time interval between the completion of what you say and your signal.

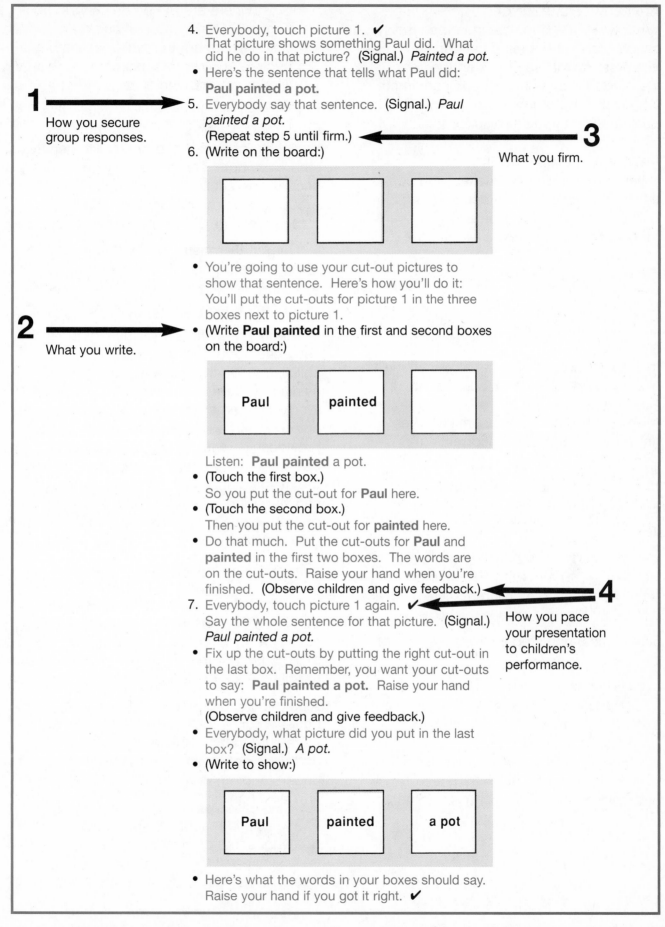

4. Everybody, touch picture 1. ✔
   That picture shows something Paul did. What did he do in that picture? (Signal.) *Painted a pot.*
• Here's the sentence that tells what Paul did:
   Paul painted a pot.

1 ──────────▶

How you secure group responses.

5. Everybody say that sentence. (Signal.) *Paul painted a pot.*
   (Repeat step 5 until firm.) ◀─────────

3

What you firm.

6. (Write on the board:)

• You're going to use your cut-out pictures to show that sentence. Here's how you'll do it: You'll put the cut-outs for picture 1 in the three boxes next to picture 1.

2 ──────────▶

What you write.

• (Write **Paul painted** in the first and second boxes on the board:)

Paul	painted	

   Listen: **Paul painted** a pot.
• (Touch the first box.)
   So you put the cut-out for **Paul** here.
• (Touch the second box.)
   Then you put the cut-out for **painted** here.
• Do that much. Put the cut-outs for **Paul** and **painted** in the first two boxes. The words are on the cut-outs. Raise your hand when you're finished. (Observe children and give feedback.) ◀─────

4

How you pace your presentation to children's performance.

7. Everybody, touch picture 1 again. ✔
   Say the whole sentence for that picture. (Signal.) *Paul painted a pot.*
• Fix up the cut-outs by putting the right cut-out in the last box. Remember, you want your cut-outs to say: **Paul painted a pot.** Raise your hand when you're finished.
   (Observe children and give feedback.)
• Everybody, what picture did you put in the last box? (Signal.) *A pot.*
• (Write to show:)

Paul	painted	a pot

• Here's what the words in your boxes should say. Raise your hand if you got it right. ✔

ARROW 2: BOARD WORK

What you write is indicated in the display boxes of the script. In the sample exercise, you first draw three boxes on the board. Then you write in each box. Scanning the boxes shows both what you'll write and how you'll change the display.

ARROW 3: FIRMING

When children make mistakes, you correct them. A correction may occur during any part of the teacher presentation that calls for children to respond. Here are the rules for corrections:

- You correct a mistake as soon as you hear it.
- A mistake on oral responses is saying the wrong thing or not responding.

In step 5, children may not say anything or may not correctly say, "Paul painted a pot." You correct as soon as you hear the mistake. You do not wait until children finish responding before correcting.

To correct, say the correct response, and then repeat the task they missed.

Some children: *Paul is . . .*
Teacher: Paul painted a pot.
Your turn. Say that sentence. (Signal.)

Remember, wherever there's an oral task that involves all the children, there's a place where children may make mistakes.

Sometimes, one step involves a series of oral tasks.

6. Girls: Put your pencil **under** your workbook. Do it. ✔
- Boys: Hold your pencil **over** your workbook. Do it. ✔
- Listen: Girls, where is your pencil? (Signal.) *Under my workbook.*
- Boys, where is your pencil? (Signal.) *Over my workbook.*

- Girls, where are the boys' pencils? (Signal.) *Over their workbooks.*
- Boys, where are the girls' pencils? (Signal.) *Under their workbooks.*
  (Repeat step 6 until firm.)

After correcting any mistakes within this series of tasks, you would return to the beginning of step 6 and present the entire step. The note **(Repeat step __ until firm)** occurs when children must correctly produce a series of responses. When you "repeat until firm," you follow these steps:

1. Correct the mistake. (Tell the response and repeat the task that was missed.)
2. Return to the beginning of the specified step and present the entire step.

"Repeating until firm" provides information you need about the children. When the children made the mistake, you told the answer. Did they remember the answer? Would they now be able to perform the step correctly? The repeat-until-firm procedure provides you with answers to these questions. You present the context in which the mistake occurred, and the children can show you through their responses whether or not the correction worked, whether or not they are **firm.**

The repeat-until-firm direction appears only on the most critical parts of new-teaching exercises. It usually focuses on knowledge that is very important for later work. In the activity above, for instance, you want to make sure that the children understand how to follow the directions.

As a general procedure, follow the repeat-until-firm directions. However, if you're quite sure that the mistake was a "glitch" and does not mean that the children lack understanding, don't follow the repeat-until-firm direction.

The specified responses for some tasks are not what some children might say. Expect variability on some group responses. Accept any reasonable wording.

If you want to hold children to the wording that is in the script (which is not necessary for tasks that can be reasonably answered in other ways), say something like, "That's right." Then say the response you want. "Everybody, say it that way."

As a rule, if more than one answer is possible for the task you presented and you know that the children's answers are reasonable, don't bother with a correction. Just move on to the next part of the teacher script.

ARROW 4: PACING YOUR PRESENTATION

You should pace your verbal presentation at a normal speaking rate—as if you were telling somebody something important.

(**Note:** The presentation works much better and the inflections are far more appropriate if you pretend that you're talking to an **adult,** not a young child. Make your message sound important.)

The most typical mistake teachers make is going too slowly or talking as if to preschoolers.

The arrows for number 4 on the diagram show two ways to pace your presentation for activities where children write or get involved in touching or finding parts of their workbook page. The first is a note to **(Observe children and give feedback).** The second is a ✔ mark. That's a note to check what the children are doing.

A ✔ requires only a second or two. If you are positioned close to several "average performing" students, check whether they are performing. If they are, proceed with the presentation.

The **(Observe children and give feedback)** direction implies a more elaborate response. You sample more children and you give feedback, not only to individual children, but to the group. Here are the basic rules for what to do and not do when you observe and give feedback.

1. Make sure that you are not at the front of the class when you present the directions for tasks that involve observing children's performance. When you direct children to place cut-outs on their worksheet (starting with the words, "Do that much"), move from the front of the room to a place where you can quickly sample the performance of low, middle and high performers.

2. As soon as children start to work, start observing. As you observe, make comments to the whole class. Focus these comments on children who are (a) following directions, (b) working quickly, (c) working accurately. "Wow, a couple of children are almost finished. I haven't seen one mistake so far."

3. When children raise their hand to indicate that they are finished, acknowledge them. (When you acknowledge that they are finished, they are to put their hand down.)

4. If you observe mistakes, do **not** provide a great deal of individual help. Point out any mistakes, but do not do the work for the children. Point to the problem and say, "I think you made a mistake. Look at the words on the board and fix up your cutouts just like that." If children are not following instructions that you gave, tell them, "You're supposed to do the first **two** boxes. You have to listen very carefully to the instructions."

5. Do not wait for the slowest children to complete the activities before presenting the work check, during which children correct their work and fix up any mistakes. A good rule early in the program is to allow a **reasonable amount of time.** You can usually use the middle performers as a gauge for what is reasonable. As you observe that they are completing their work, announce, "Okay, you have about 10 seconds more to finish up." At the end of that time, continue in the exercise.

6. Continue to circulate among the children and make sure that they fix up any mistakes you identify.

7. If you observe a serious problem that is not unique to only the lowest performers, tell the class, "Stop. We seem to have a serious problem." Repeat the part of the exercise that gives them information about what they are to do. (**Note:** Do not provide "new teaching." Simply repeat the part of the exercise that gives them the information they need and reassign the work. "Let's see who can get it this time . . . .")

8. While children do their independent work (coloring their pictures), you may want to go over any parts of the lesson with the children who had trouble. At this time, you can show them what they did wrong. Keep your explanations simple. The more you talk, the more you'll probably confuse them. If there are serious problems, repeat the exercise that presented difficulties for the lower performers.

If children take a great deal of time cutting, coloring or drawing elements, use a timer to shape their performance. First, observe average performers and see how long it takes them to complete the tasks that are time-consuming. Use that information for establishing a baseline. If average performers take 30 seconds to cut out a picture, set the criterion for 30 seconds.

Tell children, "I'm setting the timer for 30 seconds. So you'll have to work pretty fast. But work carefully. Raise your hand when you're finished."

As children raise their hand before the timer goes off, quickly check their work and make announcements, such as, "Wow, a lot of people are working fast and carefully."

When the timer goes off, say, "Everybody who finished, raise your hand. Those are Super Stars. Next time, we'll see if we have even more Super Stars." Either allow the children who didn't finish a little more time, or present the next activity to the class with the understanding that you'll work later with the children who didn't finish.

Although this procedure may seem harsh, it will very quickly shape the performance of children who are physically capable of performing and who have no physical disability.

When performance improves and virtually all children are completing the task on time, change the criterion. "I'm not going to set the timer for 30 seconds. I'm going to make it harder and set it for 25. That's going to be really tough. Let's see who can do it."

Continue to change the criterion as children improve until they are performing at an acceptable rate.

If you follow these procedures very closely, your children will work faster and more accurately. They will also become facile at following your directions.

If you don't follow these rules, you may think that you are helping children, but you will actually be reinforcing them for behaviors that you are trying to change.

If you wait far beyond a reasonable time period before presenting the work check, you punish the higher performers and the others who worked quickly and accurately. Soon, they will learn that there is no "payoff" for doing well—no praise, no recognition—but instead a long wait while you give attention to lower performers.

If you don't make announcements about children who are doing well and working quickly, the class will not understand what's expected. Children will probably not improve much.

If you provide extensive individual help on independent work, you will actually reinforce children for not listening to your directions, for being dependent on your help. Furthermore, this dependency becomes contagious. If you provide extensive individual "guidance," it doesn't take other children in the class long to discover that they don't have to listen to your directions, that they can raise their hand and receive help, and that children who have the most serious problems receive the most teacher attention. These expectations are the opposite of the ones you want to induce. You want children to be self-reliant and to have a **reason** for learning and remembering what you say when you instruct them. The simplest reason is that they will use what they have just been shown and that those who remember will receive reinforcement.

If you provide wordy explanations and extensive reteaching to correct any problems you observe, you run the serious risk of further confusing the children. Their problem is that they didn't attend to or couldn't perform on some detail that you covered in your initial presentation. So tell them what they didn't attend to and repeat the activity (or the step) that gives them the information they need. This approach shows them how to process the information you already presented. A different demonstration or explanation, however, may not show them how to link what you said originally with the new demonstration. So go light on showing children another way.

Because Level A is carefully designed, it is possible to teach all the children the desired behaviors of self-reliance, knowledge about how to follow instructions, and the ability to work fast and accurately. If you follow the management rules outlined above, by the time the children have reached lesson 20, all children should be able to complete assigned work within a reasonable period of time, and all should have reasons to feel good about their ability to do the activities.

As they improve, you should tell them about it. "What's this? Everybody's finished with part A already? That's impressive . . . ."

That's what you want to happen. Follow the rules, and it will happen.

Tracks

This section shows the development of the major tracks in Level A. The major activities are presented. Part of the discussion includes teaching notes, which address the most common problems teachers encounter.

Following Directions

Level A is designed so that children become proficient at following directions. Although the Following-Directions activities run only through lesson 38, other activities in the program involve the types of instructions that are taught in the Following-Directions track.

In lessons 1 and 2, children follow directions involving plural words and singular words.

1. Get ready to follow some directions. Listen carefully.
2. Everybody, hold up your **hand.** ✔
   Keep holding up your hand. You are holding up your hand. What are you doing? (Signal.) *Holding up my hand.*

   (To correct, say:)
   > a. Holding up my hand. Your turn: What are you doing? (Signal.) *Holding up my hand.*
   > b. (Repeat step 2 until firm.)

3. Everybody, touch your **leg.** ✔
   Keep touching your leg. You are touching your leg.
   What are you doing? (Signal.) *Touching my leg.*
   - Everybody, touch your **nose.** ✔
     Keep touching your nose.
     What are you doing? (Signal.) *Touching my nose.*
   - Girls: touch your **ears.** ✔
     What are you doing? (Signal.) *Touching my ears.*
   - Boys: touch your **knees.** ✔
     What are you doing? (Signal.) *Touching my knees.*

- Everybody, hold up your **hands.** ✔
  What are you doing? (Signal.) *Holding up my hands.*
  (Repeat step 3 until firm.)
4. Good following directions.

Teaching Notes

Although these activities are easy for most children, the game is for children to follow the directions quickly and accurately. That's what you should stress. Your goal is to present the activity very fast, with all children responding correctly and quickly.

On the first day, children may be sloppy. Reinforce children who respond quickly and accurately. If the children's performance is sloppy, repeat the activity until they are firm. Make it a game. "You can do better than that." Or, "We have some children who can follow those directions really well. Let's do it again and see who the good direction-followers are . . . ." When children do it correctly, let them know that they did well: "That's the way to follow directions. I'm impressed."

In lessons 1 and 2, children also make check marks next to numbers that you specify. Here's part of the activity from lesson 1.

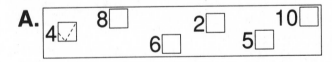

2. For some things you'll be doing in your workbook, you'll have to find the right numbers or letters.
   - Everybody, find the big box with the numbers in it. That's part A. ✔

- Touch the first number in the box. ✔
  That's a four.
  Everybody, what number? (Signal.)
  Four.
- Touch the number next to four. ✔
  Everybody, what number? (Signal.)
  Eight.
- Touch the next number. ✔
  Everybody, what number? (Signal.) *Six.*

3. Who can read all the numbers in the
   box, starting with four? (Call on several
   children. Praise responses such as: *4,
   8, 6, 2, 5, 10.*)

4. Listen: I'm going to tell you a number
   that is in the box. See how long it takes
   for you to find it.
   - Everybody, touch number **six.**
     Raise your hand when you've found it.
     **(Praise children who find the number
     within 4 seconds.)**
   - Everybody, touch number **two.**
     Raise your hand when you've
     found it. ✔
   - Everybody, touch number **eight.**
     Raise your hand when you've
     found it. ✔
   - Everybody, touch number **five.**
     Raise your hand when you've
     found it. ✔

5. You're going to make check marks.
   I'll show you how to do it.
   (Make 3 check marks on the board:)

   ✔ ✔ ✔

   - That's how to make check marks.

6. Get your pencils ready.
   You're going to put a check mark in
   the box next to the numbers I tell you
   to find.
   - Everybody, touch number **four.** ✔
     There's already a dotted check mark in
     that box.
   - Trace the check mark next to the four. ✔

7. Listen: Make a check mark in the box
   for number **eight.** Raise your hand
   when you're finished.
   (Observe children and give feedback.)

- Listen: Make a check mark in the box
  for number **two.** Raise your hand when
  you're finished.
  (Observe children and give feedback.)
- Listen: Make a check mark in the box
  for number **ten.** Raise your hand when
  you're finished.
  (Observe children and give feedback.)

8. You did a really good job of following
   instructions.
   Everybody, put your pencils down.

Teaching Notes

For this type of activity, *do not*
present from the front of the room.
Circulate among the children as
you present and give the kind of
feedback that will change their
behavior positively—that will make
them faster and more accurate.

To do that, comment on children
who are performing well. In step 4,
you tell the children, "I'm going to
tell you a number that is in the box.
See how long it takes for you to find
it. Everybody, touch number six."

Start moving and commenting.
"Wow, some children have found it
already. Look at the hands that are
up." Acknowledge the hands so that
children don't continue to hold them
up. A good procedure is to look at
the children who have their hand
raised and nod. Children can then
put their hand down.

Do not check every child's response
before presenting the next task. But
move to a different group of children,
so that you can observe as you
present. **Keep the activity moving.**

Follow this general rule throughout the program. And remember not to punish most of the children for a few. If a few children require too much time to find things or to complete their work, don't keep the other children waiting. Instead, arrange a time when you can work with the slower children separately. In the meantime, keep the activity moving, but make sure that all the children who are capable of performing have completed a task before you present the next task.

A lot of the Following-Directions activities involve coloring. Here's an activity from lesson 4.

- You're going to follow coloring rules for the numbers in the box. You'll need a yellow crayon and a brown crayon. Take out a yellow crayon and a brown crayon. Raise your hand when you're ready. ✔
2. Listen to this rule: The box next to **seven** should be yellow. Listen again: The box next to **seven** should be yellow.
- Everybody, say that rule. (Signal.) *The box next to seven should be yellow.*
- You're going to make a little yellow mark in the box next to seven. Don't color the whole box. Just put a little yellow mark in it to show that the box should be yellow. Raise your hand when you're finished. (Praise children who perform within a few seconds.)
3. Here's another coloring rule: The box next to the **cat** should be brown. Listen again: The box next to the **cat** should be brown.
- Everybody, say that rule. (Signal.) *The box next to the cat should be brown.*

- Make a brown mark in the box next to the cat. Raise your hand when you're finished. (Praise children who perform within a few seconds.)
4. Here's another coloring rule: The box next to **five** should be brown. Listen again: The box next to **five** should be brown.
- Everybody, say that rule. (Signal.) *The box next to five should be brown.*
- Make a brown mark in the box next to five. Raise your hand when you're finished. (Praise children who perform within a few seconds.)
5. Here's the last coloring rule: You can make the boxes that don't have any marks in them any color you want.
- Do it now. Fix up all the boxes so they are the right colors. Remember, if a box has a **yellow** mark in it, make the box **yellow.** If a box has a **brown** mark in it, make the box **brown.** If a box doesn't have any mark in it, make it **any color** you want. Raise your hand when you're finished.
(Observe children and give feedback. Praise children who work quickly and carefully.)
6. You did a great job of following instructions.

More complicated directions are introduced in lessons 6–9. Here's an example from lesson 9.

1. Everybody, let's see how well you can follow directions. These are tough. Take out an orange crayon, a green crayon and a brown crayon. Orange, green and brown. Do it fast. ✔
(Praise children who respond quickly.)

2. Listen: You're going to put the crayons that are **not** green under your desk.
   - Listen again: The crayons that are **not** green under your desk. Do it. ✔
   - Good following directions.
   - Listen: Where did you put the crayons that are **not** green? (Signal.) *Under my desk.*
   - What color crayons did you put under your desk? (Signal.) *Orange and brown.*
   - Crayons on your desk. ✔

3. This next one is really tough.
   - Listen: You're going to hold the crayons that are **not** brown over your desk and the other crayon on your knee.
   - Listen again: Crayons that are **not** brown over your desk. The other crayon on your knee. Do it. ✔

   (Children respond by holding green and orange crayons over their desks and brown crayon on one knee.)

   - Everybody, where is your green crayon? (Signal.) *Over my desk.*
   - Where is your orange crayon? (Signal.) *Over my desk.*
   - Where is your brown crayon? (Signal.) *On my knee.*
   - Crayons on your desk. ✔

4. Boys: You're going to put the crayon that is **not** brown **and** is **not** green on the floor.
   - Listen again: You're going to put the crayon that is **not** brown **and** is **not** green on the floor. Do it. ✔
   (Boys respond by putting orange crayon on the floor.)
   - Boys: What color is the crayon on the floor? (Signal.) *Orange.*
   - Super job! That was good thinking. Crayons on your desk.

5. Girls: You're going to hold crayons next to your head. Remember, next to your head. The crayons are **not** brown. **Not** brown. Do it.
   (Girls respond by holding green and orange crayons next to their heads.)
   - Boys: You're going to hold a crayon over your head. Remember, over your head. That crayon is **not** green **and** is **not** orange. It's **not** green **and not** orange. Do it.
   (Boys respond by holding brown crayon over their heads.)
   - Girls: Where are your crayons? (Signal.) *Next to my head.*
   - What colors are those crayons? (Signal.) *Green and orange.*
   - Boys: Where is your crayon? (Signal.) *Over my head.*
   - What color is that crayon? (Signal.) *Brown.*

6. You are really good at following very hard directions. I can't fool you.

Teaching Notes

Make sure that children wait for you to say, "Do it," before they carry out the directions.

Also, make sure that you stress the words that appear in **boldface.** These directions are difficult, but if you present them as if they are hard and praise the children who respond quickly, children will perform very well.

(**Note:** When you ask questions that cannot be answered in unison, do not be concerned about the response. For instance, if you ask, "What color crayons did you put under your desk?" and some children say, "brown and orange" [instead of "orange and brown"], accept the response. You are not relying on the verbal response to judge how well they did the task. You can see where the crayons are.)

In lessons 25–38, the Following-Directions activities involve left and right. Children work on two different notions—moving to the right or left, and turning to the right or left. To demonstrate some of these actions, you show the children how to do them or you present actions that they describe. For these models, you must face the same direction the children are facing. If you face the children, your left will be their right, and the demonstration will be very confusing—possibly disastrous. Here's the exercise for lesson 26.

1. You've learned about your right and your left.
- Everybody, hold up your **right** hand. Your **right** hand. ✔
Hands down.
- Hold up your **left** hand. Your **left** hand. ✔
Hands down.

- Touch your **right** ear. Your **right** ear. ✔
- Touch your **left** ear. Your **left** ear. ✔
Hands down.
2. Everybody, stand up. ✔
- Hold your **left** hand out to the side. ✔
- Look at your **left** hand. ✔
- Turn a corner to the **left.** ✔
- Put your left hand down. ✔
3. Everybody, hold your **right** hand out to the side. ✔
- Turn a corner to the **right.** ✔
- Everybody, sit down. ✔
4. Now you're going to tell me what I'm doing. (Turn so you face the **same** direction the children are facing, with your **back** to them.)
- I'll turn. You tell me which way I turn. Watch. (Turn **right.**)
- Everybody, which way did I turn? (Signal.) *Right.*
- Watch again. (Turn **left.**) Which way did I turn? (Signal.) *Left.*
- Watch again. (Turn **left** again.) Which way did I turn? (Signal.) *Left.*
- Watch again. (Turn **right.**) Which way did I turn? (Signal.) *Right.*
5. Good telling about right and left.

Again, it's important to maintain good pacing, but do not permit children to respond before you've asked a question or given instructions.

The purpose of the Following-Directions track is to establish "ground rules" for what children are expected to do in all activities. They are to listen to the instructions and follow them. This is not a heavy-handed rule. It's particularly important in *Reasoning and Writing A* because children have a lot of fun with parts of the program. If they treat everything as fun, they won't learn well because they won't participate in much of what is required to teach them. So the lessons should be presented as challenging, "tough" activities, some of which are a lot of fun.

True/False

Objectives for the True/False activities describe sophisticated logical operations. Much of what the children do in the track revolves around the concepts **all, some** and **none.** Children are presented with a display that shows a group of objects, such as a group of birds or a group of balloons. For some activities, children make a statement that is true about all, some or none of the objects. "All of the birds are white." They then make that statement false by changing the picture. In this case, alternative solutions are possible. They could make the statement false by making **some** of the birds a color other than white, or they could make it false by making **all** the birds a color other than white. After they change the display, a new statement is true about the display: "Some of the birds are white," or "None of the birds are white."

Other variations go in the opposite direction. The teacher makes a false statement about the picture. "All of the birds are black." Children make that statement true by changing the picture.

For many of the True/False activities, children also answer a series of questions by circling **true** or **false.** "Before you changed the picture, none of the birds were black. Circle **true** or **false** . . . ."

"After you changed the picture, none of the birds were white. True or false?"

Although these activities indeed involve complex higher-order thinking skills, the teaching is very manageable. The introduction to different types of "true/false" applications begins with simple tasks and is developed in small increments.

In lesson 1, children circle pictures to indicate which actions an animal can do or can't do. In lesson 2, this format is extended to true and false. Here's part of the worksheet and the teacher's script.

C.

1. (Write on the board:)

true   false

   - These two words are under each picture in part C of your workbook.
   - (Touch **true** on the board.)
     This word is **true.**
     (Touch **false.**)
     This word is **false.**
   - (Touch **true.**) What's this word?
     (Signal.) *True.*
     (Touch **false.**) What's this word?
     (Signal.) *False.*
2. Everybody, find the pictures of the horse. That's part C. ✔
   - Touch the words under picture 1. ✔
   - Everybody, what's the first word?
     (Signal.) *True.*
   - What's the other word? (Signal.) *False.*
3. Everybody, pick up your pencil. Look at picture 1. ✔
   - What's the horse doing in that picture? (Signal.) *Climbing a tree.*
   - Listen: Can a horse **really** climb a tree? (Signal.) *No.*
   - So circle the word **false.** The face above that word looks like this: (frown). The face shows that a horse can't **really** climb a tree.
     (Observe children and give feedback.)
4. Everybody, touch picture 2. ✔
   - What's the horse doing in that picture? (Signal.) *Eating grass.*
   - Listen: Can a horse **really** eat grass? (Signal.) *Yes.*
     So circle the word **true.** The face above that word looks like this: (smile). The face shows that a horse really can eat grass.
     (Observe children and give feedback.)

5. Everybody, touch picture 3. ✔
• What's the horse doing in that picture?
  (Signal.) *Driving a car.*
• Listen: Can a horse **really** drive a car?
  (Signal.) *No.*
• So what word are you going to circle?
  (Signal.) *False.*
• Yes, circle the word **false.** That's the
  frowning face.
  (Observe children and give feedback.)

Teaching Notes

The presentation does not assume
that children can read **true** and
false. On the workbook page, the
words are prompted with the smiling
face for **true** and the frowning face
for **false.** These prompts appear
through lesson 8, after which it is
assumed that the children can read
the words (or understand that the
word **true** always appears first).

True/False activities similar to the one above
are presented through lesson 11. In lesson
14, children apply what they have learned
about all, some and none, about true/false,
and about following directions to perform
on an activity that requires them to identify
true statements (involving all, some and
none), to say true statements, and to follow
a coloring rule for different pictures.

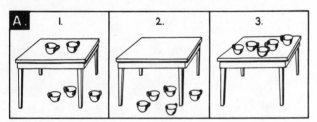

• I'm going to say statements that are
  true about one of the pictures. You
  have to find the right picture.
2. Listen: **All** of the cups are on the table.
   Everybody, say that statement. (Signal.)
   All of the cups are on the table.
• That statement is **true** about one of the
  pictures. Touch that picture. ✔

• You touched a picture that has a
  number at the top of it.
  Everybody, what's the number for the
  picture you touched? (Signal.) *Three.*
• Yes, picture 3 shows: **All** of the cups
  are on the table.
3. Here's a new statement. Listen:
   Some of the cups are on the table.
   Everybody, say that statement. (Signal.)
   Some of the cups are on the table.
• That statement is **true** about one of the
  pictures. Touch that picture. ✔
• Look at the number at the top of the
  picture. Everybody, what's the number
  for the picture you touched? (Signal.)
  One.
• Yes, picture 1 shows: **Some** of the
  cups are on the table.
4. Here's another statement. Listen:
   None of the cups are on the table.
   Everybody, say that statement. (Signal.)
   None of the cups are on the table.
• Touch the right picture. ✔
  Everybody, what's the number for the
  picture you touched? (Signal.) *Two.*
• Yes, picture 2 shows: **None** of the cups
  are on the table.
5. Your turn to say statements that are
   true about the pictures.
• Touch picture 1. ✔
  Everybody, say the statement that is
  true about picture 1. (Signal.) *Some of
  the cups are on the table.*
• Touch picture 2. ✔
  Everybody, say the statement that is
  true about picture 2. (Signal.) *None of
  the cups are on the table.*
• Touch picture 3. ✔
  Everybody, say the statement that is
  true about picture 3. (Signal.) *All of the
  cups are on the table.*
6. Who can say the statements that are
   true about all three pictures?
• (Call on several children:) Touch each
  picture and say the statement that
  is **true.**
  (Praise children who correctly say all
  three statements.)

7. Listen: You'll need your **red** crayon, **green** crayon and **blue** crayon again. ✔

• Here's a coloring rule for the cups in one of the pictures. Listen: The cups should be **red** for the picture that shows: **All** of the cups are on the table. Find the right picture and put a little red mark on one of the cups. That tells you that the cups should be red in that picture. Raise your hand when you're finished.
(Observe children and give feedback.)

8. Here's a coloring rule for the cups in another picture. Listen: The cups should be **green** for the picture that shows: **None** of the cups are on the table. Find the right picture and put a little green mark on one of the cups. Raise your hand when you're finished.
(Observe children and give feedback.)

9. Here's the coloring rule for the cups in the last picture: The cups should be **blue** for the picture that shows: **Some** of the cups are on the table. Find the right picture and put a little blue mark on one of the cups. Raise your hand when you're finished.
(Observe children and give feedback.)

10. Later you can color the cups in each picture.

Teaching Notes

This type of complex activity is typical of the program. Children use all the information that has been taught in different contexts. Earlier, the discussion for Following Directions indicated that directions are used in different tracks after they have been taught. Here's an example that points out why it was important earlier to make sure that, if the directions said, "Put a colored mark on the object," the children didn't color the entire object. For the True/False activity, it would take a fair amount of time for the children to

color all the objects. That's why the "colored mark" directions were taught earlier, even though it would not have taken the children much time to color the single boxes presented in the early Following-Directions activities.

For the next few lessons (including lesson 14), children make true statements about different pictures. These statements use the words **all, some** and **none.** Lesson 18 introduces the first activity involving changing a picture to make a different statement true about the picture. The children are given general directions about how to do it. Here's the first part of the exercise from lesson 18.

We're going to play a tough game. You're really going to have to listen and think.

2. Look at the **fours** in the box. I'm going to say some statements about the **fours** and the **check marks** next to them. You tell me if each statement is **true** or **false.**

• Listen: **All** of the fours have a check mark next to them. True or false? (Signal.) *False.*

• Listen: **Some** of the fours have a check mark next to them. True or false? (Signal.) *True.*

• Listen: **None** of the fours have a check mark next to them. True or false? (Signal.) *False*

• Everybody, say the statement that is **true** about the fours. (Signal.) *Some of the fours have a check mark next to them.*

3. Now look at the **stars** and the **check marks.** Raise your hand when you can say the statement that is **true** about the stars. ✔
- Everybody, say the statement that is **true** about the stars. (Signal.) *Some of the stars have a check mark next to them.*

4. Look at the **fours** again. Listen to the **true** statement about the **fours:** Some of the fours have a check mark next to them. You're going to fix up the fours so a **different** statement is **true.** And you're going to do that by making check marks. Listen: Fix up the fours so **all** of the fours have a check mark next to them. Use your pencil. Make your check marks. Raise your hand when you're finished.
(Observe children and give feedback.)
- Did you fix up your box so that **all** of your fours have a check mark next to them? (Signal.) *Yes.*

5. Listen to this statement: **Some** of the fours have a check mark next to them. Everybody, is that statement **now** true or false? (Signal.) *False.*
Right. You made it **false.**
- Say the statement that is **now** true about the fours. (Signal.) *All of the fours have a check mark next to them.*

If a child makes the mistake of not making check marks so that all the fours have a check mark next to them, tell the child, "Look at your fours and say the statement that's true about the fours." (Some of the fours have a check mark next to them.)

"That's the statement that was true when you started, but you were supposed to fix up the fours so that another statement is true. Fix it up so you can't say: **Some of the fours have a check mark next to them.**"

Make sure that children answer the questions in step 5 correctly. In later exercises, children will write answers to questions like the ones you present in step 5. The present exercise provides pre-teaching for the later exercises.

In later lessons, children work on different variations of the activity above. They draw things to make "some statements" true and "all statements" true. The most difficult exercise involves changing a picture that shows **all** to a picture that shows **some.** That type of exercise is introduced in lesson 31. Here's the first part of that exercise.

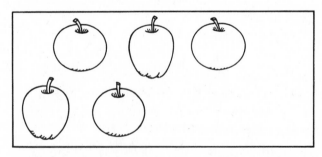

2. I'll say some statements about the picture. You listen and tell me the statement that is true.
- Listen: **All** of the apples have a stem. **Some** of the apples have a stem. **None** of the apples have a stem.

- Everybody, say the statement that is **true.** (Signal.) *All of the apples have a stem.*

3. You're going to make **this** statement true: **Some** of the apples have a stem. That's tough. Listen again: **Some** of the apples have a stem.

- Draw something in your picture so that when you're done, some of the apples **have** a stem and some of the apples do **not** have a stem. Raise your hand when you're finished.
(Observe children and give feedback.)

- Listen: Who drew some apples that do **not** have a stem? ✔

- That's what you should have done— drawn some apples that do **not** have a stem.

Teaching Notes

Some children may have trouble with the solution—drawing apples that do not have stems. Anticipate this problem. When you give instructions in step 3, stress what they are to do. "**Draw something in your picture** so that, when you're done, some of the apples have a stem and some of the apples do not have a stem."

To help children who have trouble, say, "You have to draw something in your picture. What are you going to draw? You'll draw apples. Will the apples you draw have a stem?"

Some of the True/False activities are easier. These are tasks that involve attributes of a single person or object. Here's an activity from lesson 32.

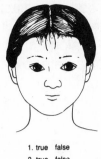

1. true false
2. true false
3. true false
4. true false

For this picture, you tell the children that three things are wrong with the picture. The girl should be smiling. The girl should be wearing glasses. Her hair should be in two long braids. The children fix up the picture to meet these criteria. Then you present a series of statements that describes the picture before the children changed it. "Before you changed the picture, the girl was smiling." "Before you changed the picture, the girl did not have glasses." The children circle **true** or **false** for each statement.

The children should not have trouble with any parts of these activities.

Later activities involving True/False are presented as "Alternative Solutions." These activities are similar to the ones described above. They involve all, some and none. They involve changing the picture. However, the Alternative-Solution problems involve a choice about how to change the picture. By exercising different options, different statements are true after the picture is changed. Alternative Solutions are described later in this guide on page 67.

Sequencing

Like Following Directions and True/False, the Sequencing activities are taught first as isolated activities. After children have practiced with the different types of Sequencing activities, sequencing becomes incorporated into other activities.

Four types of Sequencing activities are introduced in Level A. The first type is a series of pictures along an arrow showing the actions children are to perform. The first picture shows the first action, the second picture shows the second action, and so forth.

A variation of the arrow task involves pictures in a circle. The teacher demonstrates a sequence of three actions. The children label the appropriate pictures 1, 2, 3 to show the order in which the actions were presented.

The third type of Sequencing activity is a single picture with numbers that show the different places a character goes. The numbers serve as a basis for the children retelling the sequence of events. A variation of this activity involves the teacher telling the story and the children writing the numbers.

The final type of Sequencing task involves an interaction of two or more characters that are shown in a single picture. This type is the most complicated because the first thing that happens involves one illustrated character, and the next thing that happens may involve the second illustrated character. Children are shown how to "map" the actions of the characters and retell the story.

The primary focus of the Sequencing activities is to provide children with strategies that help them recount a sequence of events in different contexts.

For the first activities (beginning in lesson 1), children perform a sequence of actions that are illustrated on an arrow. Children also identify whether a sequence shown by the teacher corresponds to the picture sequence.

B.

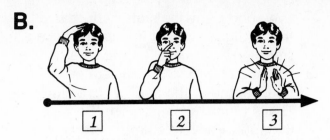

1. Everybody, find the pictures on the arrow. That's part B. ✔
• Pretend that those pictures are pictures of you. These three pictures show the things you're going to do.
2. Everybody, touch picture 1. ✔
What are you doing in that picture? (Signal.) *Touching my head.*
• Touch picture 2. ✔
What are you doing in that picture? (Signal.) *Touching my nose.*
• Touch picture 3. ✔
What are you doing in that picture? (Signal.) *Clapping.*
3. I can do all those things from the numbers.
• Here's number 1. (Touch your head.)
• Here's number 2. (Touch your nose.)
• Here's number 3. (Clap.)
4. Let's do it together.
• Do number 1.
(Touch your head as children respond.)
• Do number 2.
(Touch your nose as children respond.)
• Do number 3.
(Clap as children respond.)
5. Your turn: Don't look at your book. See if you can do all those things when I say the numbers.
• Listen: Do number 1.
(Children touch their heads.)
• Do number 2.
(Children touch their noses.)
• Do number 3.
(Children clap. Praise children who do all three things in order.)
6. Your turn to do it again. Then I'll see if I can fool you.

7. Listen: Do number 1.
(Children touch their heads.)
   - Do number 2.
(Children touch their noses.)
   - Do number 3.
(Children clap.)
(Repeat step 7 until firm.)
8. Now I'll see if I can fool you. Watch carefully. Say **wrong** if I do anything wrong.
9. Here's number 1. (Touch your knee.)
(Praise children who say: *Wrong.*)
   - Everybody, show me what I **should** do for number 1. (Children touch their heads.)
   - I'll start over.
   - Here's number 1. (Touch your head.)
   - Here's number 2. (Touch your nose.)
   - Here's number 3. (Touch your knee.)
(Praise children who say: *Wrong.*)
   - Everybody, show me what I **should** do for number 3.
(Children clap.)
(Repeat step 9 until firm.)
   - I couldn't fool you. Great job.
10. Who can say the three numbers and do the whole thing the right way? Remember to say the number and show what you do for that number. (Call on several children. Praise children who do the three actions as they say: *1, 2, 3* or *number 1, number 2, number 3.*)

Teaching Notes

Steps 7 and 9 are followed by the note, "Repeat step __ until firm." Follow these firming notes very strictly during the early parts of the program so you can see which children are having trouble.

In step 7, watch for children who are *being led* by other children. These children are possibly in trouble. If you find that some children are responding immediately and others are following, the followers may be in trouble. They may be simply learning to copy the responses of other children. Repeat the step and tell the children that they should respond right away. Do number 1. Praise children who respond immediately.

"She really listens and knows how to do it."

"Everybody, starting over. Do number 1. Wow, everybody did it that time. Do number 2."

If you don't make it clear very early in the program that you reinforce children who initiate the actions (and don't copy from others), some of the children may have serious problems later in the program. Conversely, if you set up the rules early and don't overlook non-respondents and followers, the children will learn far more quickly and will have fewer problems later in the program.

In later lessons, children practice different variations of the lesson 1 activity. For some, children write numbers to show the order of pictures along an arrow.

In lesson 7, children are introduced to the first sequencing activity that presents a single picture with numbers. The teacher describes what happens within the scene. Children touch the numbers. Then children retell the sequence by moving to the numbers in order and telling what happens at each number.

I'm going to tell you a story about a girl named Rita. You're going to touch the circles I tell you about. Then I'll see who can tell the story to me.

- Listen: Rita is trying to get across the stream without getting wet. So here's what she does first: She backs up.
- Everybody, what does she do first? (Signal.) *Backs up.*
2. One of the circles shows where she goes when she backs up. Touch the circle that shows where she is when she backs up. ✔
- Everybody, what number is in that circle? (Signal.) *One.*
That's what Rita does first.
3. After Rita backs up, she runs to the bank of the stream.
- Everybody, what does she do? (Signal.) *Runs to the bank of the stream.*
- Touch the circle that shows where she is when she's at the bank of the stream. ✔
- Everybody, what number is in that circle? (Signal.) *Two.*
4. Let's go back to the beginning. First Rita backs up. Touch the circle. ✔
- Then Rita runs to the bank. Touch the circle. ✔

- Now Rita jumps and lands on the big rock in the middle of the stream.
- Everybody, where does she land? (Signal.) *On the big rock.*
- Touch the circle that shows where she lands. ✔
Everybody, what number is in that circle? (Signal.) *Three.*
5. Then Rita jumps from the big rock and lands on the **other** bank of the stream. She lands on the **other** bank of the stream.
- Everybody, where does she land? (Signal.) *On the other bank of the stream.*
- Touch the circle that shows where she lands. ✔
- Everybody, what number is in that circle? (Signal.) *Four.*
6. I'll say the whole thing. Touch the right circles.
- **First,** Rita backs up. What number is in the circle? (Signal.) *One.*
- **Next,** Rita runs to the bank. What number is in the circle? (Signal.) *Two.*
- **Next,** Rita jumps and lands on the big rock. What number is in the circle? (Signal.) *Three.*
- **Next,** Rita jumps from the big rock and lands on the other bank of the stream. What number is in the circle? (Signal.) *Four.*
7. Let's see who can tell the story without making any mistakes. Remember, you have to tell what Rita did at each number.
- (Call on a child:) You tell the story. Everybody else, touch the numbers and make sure that (child's name) tells the right thing for each number.
(Praise child for telling what happened at each circle. Repeat with several children.)
8. Everybody, I'm going to ask you some hard questions about Rita.
- Touch the circle that shows Rita on the rock. ✔
- Everybody, what number is in the circle you're touching? (Signal.) *Three.*

- Now touch the circle that shows where Rita went just **after** she was on the rock. ✔
- Everybody, what number is in the circle you're touching? (Signal.) *Four.*
- Now touch the circle that shows where Rita was when she backed up. ✔
- Everybody, what number is in the circle you're touching? (Signal.) *One.*
- Now touch the circle that shows where Rita went just **after** she backed up. ✔
- Everybody, what number is in the circle you're touching? (Signal.) *Two.*
9. Later you can color the picture of Rita.

Teaching Notes

This activity is possibly more difficult than it looks. The reason is that children must mentally alter the picture to figure out what Rita did. The picture shows her standing close to the bank. But the numbers suggest her doing other things and being in other places. Don't be surprised if some children have trouble recounting the story in step 7. If a child has trouble telling the story, prompt by telling the child to touch the next number (or touch number 3) and tell what happened at that number.

If a lot of children have trouble recounting the story or answering the questions in step 8, repeat the activity at another time, possibly before the next lesson. Tell the children, "This is tough. Let's see who can do all the hard things I tell you to do . . . ."

Beginning in lesson 13, children write numbers to show the sequence of events in a story the teacher tells. (In lesson 13, the teacher tells a story about Paul painting a purple parrot.)

During the first reading of the story, children touch the circles that show where the paint dripped first, next and so forth. Then children write the appropriate numbers in the circles. Children retell the story and then color all the things Paul painted purple.

Teaching Notes

Children's interest in the story generally assures that they will attend to the details. However, when presenting the activity, it's a good idea to circulate among the children to make sure they are touching the appropriate places and later writing the numbers appropriately.

The final Sequencing activity occurs in lesson 46. This activity is the most difficult introduced in Level A. Children must attend to the sequence of actions and recall who did each action.

Children first listen to the story and write numbers in the appropriate circles for each action. Then they draw a path for the character who did that action—a gray path for Andrea, a yellow path for Sweetie.

The events are: Andrea hid behind the scratching post.

Sweetie walked to the opposite side of the scratching post.

Sweetie went to the bed and went to sleep.

Andrea climbed to the top of the post.

Andrea jumped onto the table.

Andrea went over to the peanuts. (No circle shown.)

After children have completed their path for Andrea and their path for Sweetie, they retell the story by starting with number 1, then going to number 2, and so on. At each number, the children tell who did something. That information comes from the color of the path to that number.

This activity provides an excellent review item because it requires children to organize their thoughts so they name the character and tell the action. The more practice they receive with this type of organization, the easier the writing assignments in Levels B and C will be for them.

If-Then

If-then reasoning is important for different decision-making situations. "If I do this . . . what will happen?" This type of if-then is the most common in everyday situations. It is causal, based on the idea that if thing 1 is done, then thing 2 will (or may) follow. The events happen in time.

A different type of if-then involves properties of related events. If number A is more than 1, then it can't be less than 1. All if-thens are based on the idea that the second thing doesn't happen unless the first happens.

Level A introduces children to both these variations of if-then. The general format involves two pictures on an arrow: The first picture shows the "if" part; the second picture shows the "then" part. The "if" part is first introduced with actions: "If the teacher claps, touch your head."

Other variations of if-then activities involve statements containing the words **and, or.**

Extended if-thens involve two arrows. The first arrow generates one if-then; the second arrow generates the second if-then. These activities demonstrate to children an if-then chain. If Clarabelle goes on the diving board, the diving board will break. If the diving board breaks, Clarabelle will fall into the pool.

Children are also shown how to relate if-then reasoning to static features of objects. These activities involve two arrows. The first arrow shows a series of objects that vary in a particular dimension (circles of increasing size). The second arrow shows a correlated set of events (triangles getting darker). Children construct if-thens for these displays. If the circles get bigger, the triangles get darker. Children work a variety of activities that require them to construct the examples for rules.

If-thens are first introduced in lesson 6. Here's the introduction.

- Pretend that the first picture is a picture of me and the next picture is a picture of you. The two pictures show a rule.
2. Touch the **second** picture. Not the first picture. The second picture. ✔
- That picture shows what **you'll** do. You'll touch your head.
- Touch the **first** picture. ✔
- That picture shows what **I'll** do.
3. Listen to the rule: **If** I clap my hands, you'll touch your head.
- What are you going to do if I clap my hands? (Signal.) *Touch my head.*

- But if I do something else, you don't do anything. The **only** time you touch your head is when I clap my hands. Remember, **if** I clap my hands, you'll touch your head. If I **don't** clap my hands, you won't do anything.
4. Here we go. Watch carefully and don't get fooled.
- My turn. (Touch your head.) Your turn. (Praise children who do not respond.)
- My turn again. (Snap your fingers.) Your turn. (Praise children who do not respond.)
- My turn again. (Clap your hands.) Your turn. (Praise children who immediately touch their head.)
- My turn again. (Clap your hands.) Your turn. (Praise children who immediately touch their head.)
- My turn again. (Move your hands as if clapping, but don't clap.) Your turn. (Praise children who do not respond.)
- My turn again. (Touch your head.) Your turn. (Praise children who do not respond.)
- My turn again. (Clap your hands.) Your turn. (Praise children who immediately touch their head.)
5. (Repeat any items that children missed.)
6. You did a great job of following the rule.

Teaching Notes

This activity is fun, but it involves following directions, so make sure you praise children who do it the right way and follow your directions.

In later lessons, children are introduced to more complicated arrows. The first type involves an **and** rule. The teacher must perform both actions shown in the picture before the children respond.

Pretend that the first picture is a picture of me and that the next picture is a picture of you.

- You're going to learn a new kind of rule. It's tough. Listen to the rule: If I touch my ear **and** touch my nose, you'll stand up. Listen again: If I touch my ear **and** touch my nose, you'll stand up.

2. Everybody, touch the picture that shows what **you'll** do. ✔
- What are you doing in that picture? (Signal.) *Standing up.*

3. Everybody, touch the picture that shows what **I'll** do. ✔
- What am I doing in that picture? (Signal.) *Touching your ear and touching your nose.*

4. Listen to the rule again: If I touch my ear **and** touch my nose, you'll stand up.
- What are you going to do if I **just** touch my ear? (Signal.) *Nothing.*
- What are you going to do if I **just** touch my nose? (Signal.) *Nothing.*
- What are you going to do if I touch my ear **and** touch my foot? (Signal.) *Nothing.*
- What are you going to do if I touch my ear **and** touch my nose? (Signal.) *Stand up.*
- Remember, the only time you'll stand up is when I touch my ear **and** touch my nose.

5. Here we go. Watch carefully and don't get fooled.
- My turn. (Touch your nose.) Your turn. (Praise children who do not respond.)
- My turn again. (Simultaneously touch your ear and your head.) Your turn. (Praise children who do not respond.)
- My turn again. (Simultaneously touch your ear and your nose.) Your turn. (Praise children who immediately stand up.) Sit down.
- My turn again. "Stand up." Your turn. (Praise children who do not respond.)
- My turn again. Simultaneously touch your ear and your chin.) Your turn. (Praise children who do not respond.)
- My turn again. (Simultaneously touch your ear and your nose.) Your turn. (Praise children who immediately stand up.) Sit down again.

6. Raise your hand if you followed all those hard directions. ✔ You did a great job of following the rule. You knew just when to stand up.
- When did you stand up? (Signal.) *When you touched your ear and your nose.*

Teaching Notes

In step 3, do not require a perfect unison response. Some children may say the parts in a different order (*touching your nose and ear*). If you have doubts about whether they understand, say the answer you want them to say, like this: "Yes, touching my ear and touching my nose. Everybody, say it that way." If you're sure that the children understand, then don't require them to say it a specified way. Follow their response with, "Yes, I'm touching my ear and touching my nose." Then go on in the exercise.

Use this procedure whenever children produce a unison response that is reasonable but not as written. If you have doubts, say "Yes," and then tell them the way you want them to say it and direct them to say it that way. If you don't have doubts, say "Yes," and then say it as written in the presentation book and move on.

To keep this activity moving, it's a good idea to practice step 5 before presenting it to the children. When presenting step 5, look for the "My turns," and then mark where you'll do another action. If you lose your place in an activity like this one, don't worry. No harm occurs if you repeat a task you've already presented or if you happen to present the tasks out of order.

In lesson 15, children are introduced to **or.** The arrow shows two pictures for the teacher's actions (one over the other, with the word **or** between them). The rule is that, if the teacher does either of these actions, the children are to perform their action.

In lesson 17, children are confronted with the discrimination of **and** rules and **or** rules. The children play two games, first for the **and** rule, then for the **or** rule.

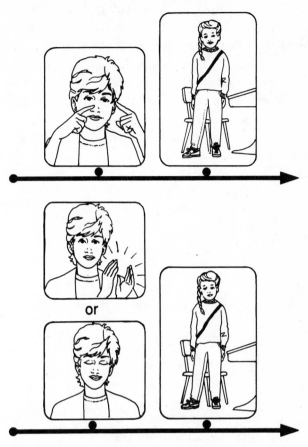

You're going to play two different games.
- The pictures for the first game are on the **top** arrow. Touch the pictures for the first game. ✔
  I'll say the rule: If I touch my ear **and** touch my nose, you'll stand up.
- The pictures for the second game are on the bottom arrow. Touch the pictures for the second game. ✔
  I'll say the rule: If I clap my hands **or** close my eyes, you'll stand up.
2. Let's see who can say the rules for the games. Who can say the rule for the **first** game—the first game? (Call on several children. Idea: *If you touch your ear **and** touch your nose, we'll stand up.*)

- Who can say the rule for the **second** game? (Call on several children. Idea: *If you clap your hands **or** close your eyes, we'll stand up.*)

3. Listen: Who can say **both** rules—the rule for the first game and the rule for the second game? (Call on several children. Idea: *If you touch your ear **and** touch your nose, we'll stand up. If you clap your hands **or** close your eyes, we'll stand up.*)
(Praise children who correctly say both rules.)

4. Everybody, touch the pictures for the **first** game. ✔
Think about what you'll do and when you'll do it. Think big, because I'm going to try to fool you. Everybody ready?
- My turn. (Touch your nose.)
Your turn. (Praise children who do not respond.)
- My turn. (Simultaneously touch your ear and your nose.)
Your turn. (Praise children who immediately stand up.)
Good. Now sit down again.
- My turn. (Touch your ear.)
Your turn. (Praise children who do not respond.)
- My turn. (Touch both ears.)
Your turn. (Praise children who do not respond.)
- My turn. "Stand up."
Your turn. (Praise children who do not respond.)
- My turn. (Simultaneously touch your ear and your nose.)
Your turn. (Praise children who immediately stand up.)
Good. Sit down again.

 (After presenting all tasks, repeat any tasks that gave children problems. Praise children who performed on all the tasks. Say:) You're really good at following the rule. I couldn't fool you.

5. Now touch the pictures for the **second** game. ✔
This is where I'm going to try to fool you. Remember, this is the **or** game. If I do either one of those two things, you should stand up. Think big. Everybody ready?
- My turn. (Close your eyes.)
Your turn. (Praise children who immediately stand up.)
Good. Sit down again.
- My turn. (Clap your hands.)
Your turn. (Praise children who immediately stand up.)
Good. Sit down again.
- My turn. "Clap your hands."
Your turn. (Praise children who do not respond.)
- My turn. "Stand up."
Your turn. (Praise children who do not respond.)
- My turn. (Clap your hands.)
Your turn. (Praise children who immediately stand up.)
Good. Sit down again.
- My turn. (Close your eyes.)
Your turn. (Praise children who immediately stand up.)
Good. Sit down again.
- (After presenting all tasks, repeat any tasks that gave children problems.)

6. Raise your hand if you got **everything** right. ✔
You're really good at following the rule. I couldn't fool you.

Teaching Notes

If children have trouble with the second game, plan to repeat the entire exercise at a later time. You can say something like, "Wow, that is hard. We'll have to try that one again later."

A similar task is presented in lesson 18, but the children will probably perform perfectly on it if they are "firmed" in the lesson 17 task. It's better to repeat the lesson 17 activity at a later time, not during the lesson. Conditional chains (more than one if-then) are introduced in lesson 34.

The two arrows show that there are two if-thens. The children first say the if-then statement for the first arrow: If Clarabelle walks out onto the diving board, the diving board will break. Then they say the if-then statement for arrow 2. This if-then starts with the second picture: If the diving board breaks, Clarabelle will fall into the water.

After children work with the two if-then statements, you direct them to say both rules.

8. Everybody, get ready to say both rules. Say the rule for arrow 1. (Signal.) *If Clarabelle walks out onto the diving board, the diving board will break.*
- Say the rule for arrow 2. (Signal.) *If the diving board breaks, Clarabelle will fall into the water.*
(Repeat step 8 until firm.)

Teaching Notes

Make sure children are firm on step 8. If some children are still making mistakes after you present step 8 two or three times, make a note of their problem, reassure them that this is a tough task and present it again at a later time (preferably before lesson 35).

The problem the children will most likely have is stating the second if-then. Remind them: "Remember, for arrow 2, you start with **if** and tell about the second picture; then tell about the third picture."

Clarabelle

In lesson 49, children are introduced to correlated changes in dimensions or properties of objects. The introduction involves a simple change across two objects—circles and triangles.

C.

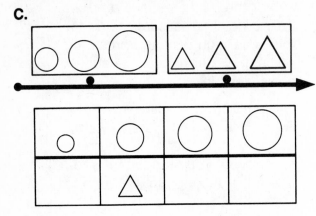

You're going to learn a new kind of **if** rule.

2. Touch the arrow in part C. ✔
   There are two boxes on that arrow.
   - Everybody, what's in the first box? (Signal.) *Circles.*
   - What's in the second box? (Signal.) *Triangles.*
3. Touch the box with circles. ✔
   Look at how those circles change as they go along the arrow.
   - Everybody, how are the circles changing? (Signal.) *They're getting bigger.*
   - Right, the circles are getting bigger and bigger.
   - Now touch the box with the triangles. ✔
     Look at how those triangles change as they go along the arrow.
   - Everybody, how are the triangles changing? (Signal.) *They're getting bigger.*
   - Right, the triangles are getting bigger and bigger.
4. See if you can help me out with the **if** rule. Here's the first part: If the circles get bigger, the triangles . . . do what? (Signal.) *Get bigger.*
   - So here's the whole rule: If the circles get bigger, the triangles get bigger.

5. Everybody, say the rule. (Signal.) *If the circles get bigger, the triangles get bigger.*
   (Repeat step 5 until firm.)
6. Now you're going to use that rule to complete the box **below** the arrow. The circles are in the **top** row.
   - What's in the **bottom** row? (Signal.) *A triangle.*
   - In the **top** row, you can see what the circles are doing. What are the circles doing? (Signal.) *Getting bigger.*
   - If the circles get bigger, then what are the triangles supposed to do? (Signal.) *Get bigger.*
   - But you can't see what all the triangles are doing because some of them are missing.
7. See if you can use the rule about the circles and triangles to put in the missing triangles. Remember, the circles are getting bigger, so the triangles have to get bigger. Fix up the triangles. Raise your hand when you're finished.
   (Observe children and give feedback.)
8. (Draw on the board:)

   △ △ △ Δ

   - Check your work. Here's what your bottom row should look like. Who got it right?
     (Children respond.)
9. Your triangles now follow a rule. Who can say the whole **if** rule? (Call on several children. Praise children who correctly say the whole rule.)

In later lessons, children work with increasingly less predictable relationships: As the stars get bigger, the circles get more dots; as the apples get bigger, the triangles get smaller; as the rats get fatter, the lines get shorter.

After this exposure, children construct their own rules. Here's the introduction of this type of activity from lesson 57.

B.

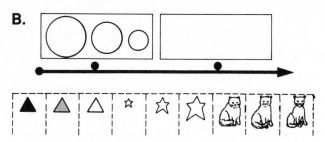

1. (Hold up a workbook. Point to cut-outs of triangles, stars and cats in part B.) We're going to play a new kind of game. Cut out all the triangles, stars and cats. Cut along all the dotted lines so you have three separate triangles, three separate stars and three separate cats. Raise your hand when you're finished.
(Observe children and give feedback.)
2. I'm going to tell you a rule. You'll put the right objects in the **second** box on the arrow to show that rule.
   • Everybody, touch the arrow. ✔
   Look at how the circles are changing. Say the first part of the **if** rule. (Signal.) *If the circles get smaller.*
   • Here's the **whole** if rule. Listen: If the circles get smaller, the triangles get darker. Listen again: If the circles get smaller, the triangles get darker.
3. Everybody, say that rule. (Signal.) *If the circles get smaller, the triangles get darker.*
   (Repeat step 3 until firm.)
4. Fix up the **second** part of your arrow so it shows the triangles getting darker. Raise your hand when you're finished.
   (Observe children and give feedback.)
5. Listen: Which triangle did you put first: the **darkest** triangle or the **lightest** triangle? (Signal.) *The lightest triangle.*

• Which triangle did you put last? (Signal.) *The darkest triangle.*
• Raise your hand if you got it right. ✔ Take your triangles off the arrow. ✔
6. Here's a new rule. Listen: If the circles get smaller, the stars get bigger.
7. Everybody, say that rule. (Signal.) *If the circles get smaller, the stars get bigger.* (Repeat step 7 until firm.)
8. Fix up the second part of the arrow so it shows that rule. Raise your hand when you're finished.
(Observe children and give feedback.)
9. Listen: Which star did you put first: the **smallest** star or the **biggest** star? (Signal.) *The smallest star.*
• And which star did you put last? (Signal.) *The biggest star.*
• Raise your hand if you got it right. ✔ Take your stars off the arrow. ✔
10. Here's a new rule: If the circles get smaller, the cats get skinnier.
11. Everybody, say that rule. (Signal.) *If the circles get smaller, the cats get skinnier.* (Repeat step 11 until firm.)
12. Fix up the arrow so it shows that rule. Raise your hand when you're finished.
(Observe children and give feedback.)
13. Listen: Which cat did you put first: the **fattest** cat or the **skinniest** cat? (Signal.) *The fattest cat.*
• Which cat did you put last? (Signal.) *The skinniest cat.*
• Raise your hand if you got it right. ✔
14. Raise your hand if you can say a rule that we haven't used with the triangles, the stars or the cats. (Call on several children. Praise rules such as: *If the circles get smaller, the triangles get lighter* or *If the circles get smaller, the stars get smaller* or *If the circles get smaller, the cats get fatter.*)

In step 3, the children know the rule they will be constructing. Do not permit children to construct the display until you tell them to.

When presenting step 3, observe the children. If some children are not following your directions, praise children who are; then tell the class that you'll have to start over. "If you have anything in your second box, remove it. Then listen carefully to the instructions. Here we go . . . ." Then repeat step 3.

Follow this same procedure at steps 7 and 11. This procedure is not based on the principle that "children must follow the teacher's instructions," but rather on the idea that, if you don't require children to respond to your directions, some of them will not learn the material, and those who do follow your directions quickly learn that they don't have to.

Note that in step 14, children can create a rule. Be prepared for some rules that you may not immediately recognize. A child may show the cats getting skinnier and leaning more to the left, or the stars getting bigger and closer together. If you don't recognize a rule, ask the child: "What's the rule for your cats?" Praise unique responses if they are consistent with the display.

Classification

Many skills and activities that children will work on in later instruction assume a knowledge of classification. Classification is a structurally difficult concept for children. The structural problem can be seen by presenting these two tasks:

"I'm thinking of a dog. Is it an animal?"
and
"I'm thinking of an animal. Is it a dog?"

The answer to the first question is **yes,** because dogs possess all the attributes of animals and they possess additional features that set them apart as a subgroup of animals—dogs. The answer to the second question is probably **no,** because there are a lot of things that have all the features of animals that are not dogs.

An objective of a program that introduces "classification" should be to teach this relationship. A further relationship that should be taught is that the basis for classification is **sameness.** Things are in the same class because they possess features that are the same for all members of the class.

Level A introduces children to various common classes, introduces the logic of sub-classes and associates classification with other skills that are taught in the program (such as following coloring rules for things that are the same or for objects that are in the same class).

Many traditional introductory activities are confusing because they start with the members of the class and try to describe the class. For instance, the teacher will state a car is a vehicle. Children already know that a car is a car. They also know that statements of the form, "A car is _____," tell about some feature of a car: "A car is made of metal, a car is something with tires . . . ," etc. Therefore, they sometimes become quite confused trying to identify the "vehicleness" in cars. The introductory activity in Level A avoids these problems. The children are first told that all the objects are vehicles. Then the children get a chance to answer questions that ask about the **kind** of vehicle. ("What kind of vehicle is that?") This order of introduction gives them a framework for understanding that all the objects are vehicles, but that each vehicle is a "familiar" kind—car, truck, bus and so forth.

The first Classification activity is presented in lesson 11.

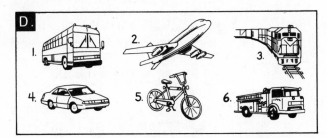

Touch the big box with the objects in it. ✔
- The objects inside the box are **vehicles.** What are they? (Signal.) *Vehicles.*
- All things in the box are vehicles. Listen: A vehicle is something made to take things places. Listen again: A vehicle is something made to take things places. What is a vehicle made to do? (Signal.) *Take things places.*

2. Touch vehicle 1. ✔
Everybody, what kind of vehicle is that? (Signal.) *A bus.*
- Touch vehicle 2. ✔
Everybody, what kind of vehicle is that? (Signal.) *An airplane.*
- Touch vehicle 3. ✔
Everybody, what kind of vehicle is that? (Signal.) *A train.*
- Touch vehicle 4. ✔
Everybody, what kind of vehicle is that? (Signal.) *A car.*
- Touch vehicle 5. ✔
Everybody, what kind of vehicle is that? (Signal.) *A bike.*
- Touch vehicle 6. ✔
Everybody, what kind of vehicle is that? (Signal.) *A fire truck.*
Yes, it's a fire truck.

3. Who can name a vehicle that is not in the box? (Call on several children. Praise appropriate responses, saying: Good, a (vehicle's name) is made to take things places so a (vehicle's name) is a vehicle.)

4. Later you can color all the vehicles.

Teaching Notes

In step 3, children name different vehicles. Make sure you follow the procedure of telling why each one is a vehicle. "Good, a wagon is made to take things places. So a wagon is a vehicle." If children propose something that is not a vehicle, such as a swing, you can apply the test to show why it is not a vehicle. "Does a swing take things places? Not really, it just goes back and forth. So a swing is not a vehicle."

Beginning with lesson 12, children follow coloring rules for classes and sub-classes. Lesson 12 involves vehicles. The rule that children apply involves all the vehicles that go on streets and roads. Here's the presentation.

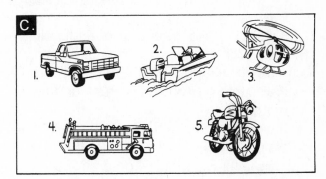

Touch the big box with the objects in it. ✔
- All those things are called something. Think. What are they all called? (Signal.) *Vehicles.*
- And what is a vehicle made to do? (Signal.) *Takes things places.*

2. Everybody, touch vehicle 1. ✔
What kind of vehicle is that? (Signal.) *A pickup truck.*
Yes, a **pickup** truck.
- Touch vehicle 2. ✔
What kind of vehicle is that? (Signal.) *A boat.*

- Touch vehicle 3. ✔
  What kind of vehicle is that? (Signal.)
  A helicopter.
- Touch vehicle 4. ✔
  What kind of vehicle is that? (Signal.)
  A fire truck.
  Yes, a **fire** truck.
- Touch vehicle 5. ✔
  What kind of vehicle is that? (Signal.)
  A motorcycle.

3. Who can name a vehicle that is not in the box? (Call on several children. Praise appropriate responses.)

4. Everybody, listen: Some of the vehicles in the box go on streets and roads. Here's the rule about those vehicles: **All** the vehicles that go on streets and roads should be **blue.** That's the rule for all the vehicles that go on streets and roads. None of the other vehicles should be blue.
- Your turn: Put a little blue mark on each vehicle that should be blue. Don't put marks on the other vehicles. Raise your hand when you're finished. (Observe children and give feedback.)

5. Name the vehicles you marked with blue. (Call on a child. Praise responses that name a truck, a fire truck and a motorcycle.)
- Raise your hand if you got them right. ✔

6. Listen: Why **didn't** you color the helicopter blue? (Call on a child. Idea: *A helicopter doesn't go on streets and roads.*)
- Why **did** you color the motorcycle blue? (Call on a child. Idea: *A motorcycle goes on streets and roads.*)

7. Everybody, later you'll color all the vehicles that should be blue. Those are the vehicles that go on streets and roads.

After the introduction to vehicles, the program presents different classes following the same basic procedure used for vehicles (animals, buildings, food, etc.).

The program introduces "descriptions" of class members as "clues" about the members. A good "clue" permits you to identify the member. Here's the introduction from lesson 38.

- These things are all in the same class. Everybody, what class is that? (Signal.) *Buildings.*

2. I'll name the buildings. You touch them.
- Touch the hardware store. ✔
- Touch the school. ✔
- Touch the movie theater. ✔
- Touch the church. ✔
- Touch the house. ✔
- Touch the barn. ✔

3. I'll tell you clues about the buildings. You're going to write the number of the clue under the correct building.
- Here's clue **1:** A lot of children go to this building to get smart. Write number 1 in the box under the building for that clue. Listen again: A lot of children go to this building to get smart. Raise your hand when you've written number 1 under the building where a lot of children go to get smart.
  (Observe children and give feedback.)
- Everybody, you wrote the number 1 under a building. Which building is that? (Signal.) *A school.*

4. Here's clue **2:** Clarabelle spends every night in this building. Write number 2 in the box under the building for that clue. Listen again: Clarabelle spends every night in this building. Raise your hand when you've written number 2 under the building where Clarabelle spends every night.
   (Observe children and give feedback.)
   - Everybody, you wrote the number 2 under a building. Which building is that? (Signal.) *A barn.*

5. Here's clue **3:** Paul buys a lot of paint in this building. Write number 3 in the box under the building for that clue. Listen again: Paul buys a lot of paint in this building. Raise your hand when you're finished writing number 3.
   (Observe children and give feedback.)
   - Everybody, you wrote the number 3 under a building. Which building is that? (Signal.) *A hardware store.*

6. Here's clue **4:** Roxie and her whole family go to this building every Sunday morning to worship. Write number 4 in the box under the building for that clue. Listen again: Roxie and her whole family go to this building every Sunday morning to worship. Raise your hand when you're finished writing number 4.
   (Observe children and give feedback.)
   - Everybody, you wrote the number 4 under a building. Which building is that? (Signal.) *A church.*

7. You have numbers under four of the pictures. But I don't have clues for the rest of them. See if you can think of a clue. Remember, you can't **name** the building. You have to tell what **happens** in that building. Raise your hand if you can say a clue about one of the buildings that doesn't have a number under it.

8. (Call on a child:) What is your clue? (For a good clue, tell the children to write number 5 under the appropriate picture.)

9. (Call on a child:) What is your clue? (For a good clue, tell the children to write number 6 under the appropriate picture.)

Teaching Notes

When this activity is introduced, children have already worked with clues in other contexts. See Questions and Clues, page 61.

Beginning with lesson 62, children do a variety of activities that involve the glossary in the back of their workbook. (Activities are also discussed under Questions and Clues, page 65.) All these activities involve classification. Some require children to indicate which members of a class a "clue" rules out. Other activities require children to use the glossary and develop clues for specified objects. These activities are valuable for extending what children know about classification because they demonstrate that objects can be "described" by their location as well as by their class features or use. The test of clues generated by children is whether the clues permit one to identify the targeted object.

Beginning with lesson 54, Level A presents a kind of detective game that involves binary logic (or classification systems that present only two choices).

In lesson 56, children are presented with the first two-rung ladder activity. Variations of this activity appear in later lessons. Here's the first part of the board demonstration from lesson 56.

1. (Draw on the board:)

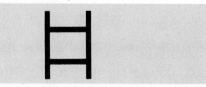

- This picture shows two rungs of a ladder. We're going to play a lot of ladder games.

- (Touch the top rung.)
  This is the **top** rung of the ladder.
- (Touch the bottom rung.)
  This is the **bottom** rung of the ladder.
2. (Touch the top rung of the ladder.)
  This rung is **just** as long as the bottom rung. But you can fix up the ladder so the top rung is **longer** than the bottom rung. And there are two ways to do it.
- I'll show you one way to fix up the ladder so the **top** rung is **longer** than the bottom rung. Watch.
- (Change picture on the board to show:)

- I did it. I fixed up the ladder so the top rung is longer than the bottom rung.
- But there's **another** way to fix up the rungs. And only really smart people know this way.
- (Erase extension to top rung to show:)

3. I'm going to fix up the ladder another way so the **top** rung is **longer** that the bottom rung. Watch.
- (Erase part of bottom rung to show:)

- That's pretty tricky, isn't it? I fixed up the ladder so the **top** rung is **longer** than the bottom rung and I didn't even do anything to the top rung.
- What did I do? (Call on a child. Idea: *Made the bottom rung shorter.*)
- What did I do the **first** time I fixed up the ladder so the top rung was longer than the bottom rung? (Call on a child. Idea: *Made the top rung longer.*)
  Right, I made the top rung longer.

Following the demonstration, children do workbook activities in which they apply the procedures to ladders in their workbook.

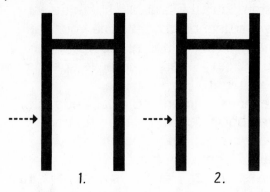

1.   2.

Children first draw the bottom rung in each ladder. They then fix up ladder 1 so the top rung is longer than the bottom rung. They do that without doing anything to the top rung. They fix up ladder 2 so the top rung is longer than the bottom rung, but they don't do anything to the bottom rung.

Beginning with lesson 61, children work similar problems involving a teeter-totter. Children learn the rule that there are two ways to make an end of a teeter-totter go down—push down on that end or push up on the other end. Here's the worksheet page from lesson 62.

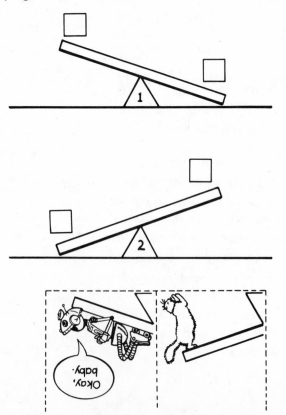

Children first draw the arrows on the teeter-totters to indicate the two ways each teeter-totter could have been moved. They also write **L** and **R** in the boxes to indicate the left side and right side.

Next, you give them information about what happened to move each teeter-totter.

5. Here's a fact about teeter-totter 1: Bleep moved the teeter-totter so the **right** end is **down**. And Bleep did **not** touch the **left** end. Listen again: Bleep did **not** touch the **left** end. Raise your hand when you know what Bleep did to move the teeter-totter. ✔
• Everybody, what did Bleep do to move the teeter-totter? (Signal.) *Pushed down on the right end.*
Yes, Bleep pushed **down** on the **right** end.

The information you give next about teeter-totter 2 is that Sweetie moved the left end down and Sweetie did not touch the left end.

At the end of the exercise, children cut out the upside-down pictures of the characters on the page and (later) paste them in place.

Right/Left

Children are taught **right** and **left** and then apply the concepts of right/left to various problems (such as the teeter-totter problem above and maze problems).

Children are taught different aspects of right/left. They are taught right/left body parts, turning to the right or left and identifying objects using "right" or "left." Some identifications involve a reference point. "Sweetie is to the **right** of the tree."

In lesson 18, **right** is introduced.

A.

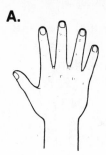

• You're going to learn which side is the **right** side of something.
2. Everybody, touch picture A. ✔
That shows a picture of a **right** hand. Put your **right** hand on top of the hand in the picture. ✔
• Everybody, now hold up your **right** hand. ✔
• Tap the back of your **right** hand with your other hand so you can feel which hand is your **right** hand. ✔
3. Everybody, you're going to touch the knee that is on the same side of your body as your right hand. That's your **right** knee. ✔
• Touch your **right** knee. ✔ (Praise children who respond correctly.)
• Touch your **right** ear. ✔
• Touch your **right** foot. ✔
4. Let's do those again.
• Everybody, hold up your **right** hand. ✔ Which hand are you holding up? (Signal.) *My right hand.*
• Touch your **right** knee. ✔
Everybody, what are you touching? (Signal.) *My right knee.*
• Touch your **right** ear. ✔
Everybody, what are you touching? (Signal.) *My right ear.*
• Touch your **right** foot. ✔
Everybody, what are you touching? (Signal.) *My right foot.*
5. Remember which hand is your **right** hand. Raise your hand if you write with your **right** hand. ✔
• When you shake hands with someone, you shake hands with your **right** hand. Later on, I'm going to shake hands with you. Remember to shake hands with your **right** hand.

Children work on **right** through lesson 25 before being introduced to **left.** The purpose of this delay is to assure that children are firm on **right** so they do not confuse right with left. Here's the introduction of **left** from lesson 25.

1. Everybody, touch your **right** ear. Your **right** ear. ✔
- Now move your hand to the **right.** ✔ Good moving to the right.
- Touch your **right** leg. Your **right** leg. ✔
- Listen: Move your **right** foot to the **right**. ✔
- Everybody, stand up and face me. ✔
- Take little steps and move to the **right.** ✔
- Everybody, sit down. ✔
- Touch your **right** knee. Your **right** knee. ✔ What are you touching? (Signal.) *My right knee.*

2. Everybody, hold up your **right** hand. ✔ Listen: Your **other** hand is your **left** hand. What's your **other** hand called? (Signal.) *My left hand.* Put your right hand down. ✔
- Everybody, hold up your **left** hand. ✔ What are you holding up? (Signal.) *My left hand.*
- Everybody, touch your **left** knee with your **left** hand. ✔ What are you touching? (Signal.) *My left knee.*

- Touch your **left** ear with your **left** hand. ✔ What are you touching? (Signal.) *My left ear.*
- Touch your **left** foot with your **left** hand. ✔ What are you touching? (Signal.) *My left foot.*

3. Listen carefully. Everybody, hold up your **right** hand. Your **right** hand. ✔ What are you holding up? (Signal.) *My right hand.* Hands down. ✔
- Everybody, hold up your **left** hand. Your **left** hand. ✔
- Everybody, hold your **left** hand out to your **left** side. ✔
- Everybody, wave with your **left** hand. Hands down. ✔

4. Raise your **left** hand if you think you'll remember your **left** hand next time. ✔

In lesson 21, children turn to the right.

5. Everybody, stand up. ✔ I'll show you how to turn to the right. **(Face the same direction the children are facing, with your back to them.)**
- First I put my right arm out to the side. **(Do it.)** Then I turn until I'm lined up with my arm. **(Turn a 90-degree corner.)**
- I don't go all the way around. I just turn like I'm going around a corner. Watch again. **(Face the same direction the children are facing, with your back to them. Turn a 90-degree corner.)**

6. Your turn: Put your arm out to the side. ✔ Now turn until you're lined up with your right arm. ✔ You just turned to the **right.**
- Get ready to turn to the right again. Hold your **right** arm out. Turn to the right. ✔
- Do it without holding your arm out. Turn to the right. ✔
- Again: Turn to the right. ✔ **(Repeat step 6 until firm.)**

7. Good turning to the right. Let's see if you can answer some questions.
- Everybody, turn to the right. ✔
What did you do? (Signal.) *Turned to the right.*
- Again: Turn to the right. ✔
What did you do? (Signal.) *Turned to the right.*
8. Good turning to the right. Will you remember how to do that? (Signal.) *Yes.*
- Everybody, sit down.

> **Teaching Notes**
>
> When children turn to the right, they may turn too far. Remind them that they're just turning a corner. To correct a child who makes this mistake, direct the child to hold her right hand to the right. (You can hold her right hand in place.) Then tell the child to turn until she is facing the same direction as her hand. (Keep her hand stationary as she turns.)
>
> You may have to give some children several demonstrations until they get the idea that their hand doesn't move and that they turn until they are facing the same direction as their hand.

Beginning in lesson 38, children work problems that involve mazes. In this exercise, rats are shown in different orientations. Children write an **R** on each rat's right front paw; then they write **R** or **L** in the circle to show the direction the rat turns.

These are pictures of the bragging rat with a long tail. You're going to figure out which way he turns at each corner.
2. Touch the picture that shows rat 1. ✔
Listen: You're going to write **R** on the bragging rat's right front paw. There's a box on the right front paw. Make an **R** in that box. Raise your hand when you're finished.
(Observe children and give feedback.)
3. Now look at the arrow that goes around the corner. That arrow shows which way the rat turns. Remember the rule: If he turns toward his **right** paw, it's a **right** turn. If he turns toward his **left** paw, it's a **left** turn.
- Everybody, which way does rat 1 turn? (Signal.) *Right.*
- Yes, he turns right. Write **R** inside the circle at that corner. The **R** shows it's a **right** turn. Raise your hand when you're finished.
(Observe children and give feedback.)

4. Touch the picture that shows rat 2. ✔
(Hold up a workbook. Turn the page so rat 2 is facing straight up.)
- Turn your page like this so rat 2 is facing straight up. Make sure his tail is the closest thing in the picture to you. The number on the rat should be right-side-up.
(Observe children and give feedback.)
- Now write **R** on the rat's **right** front paw. Raise your hand when you're finished.
(Observe children and give feedback.)

5. Now look at the arrow that goes around the corner. That arrow shows which way the rat turns. Everybody, which way does rat 2 turn? (Signal.) *Left.*
- Yes, he turns left. Write **L** inside the circle at that corner to show that he took a **left** turn. Raise your hand when you're finished.
(Observe children and give feedback.)

6. Touch the picture that shows rat 3. ✔
Turn your page so that rat 3 is facing straight up. Remember, his tail should be the closest thing in the picture to you and the number should be right-side-up.
(Observe children and give feedback.)
- Now write **R** on the rat's right front paw. Then write **R** or **L** in the circle to show if the rat turns **right** or **left.** Think big. And don't get fooled. Raise your hand when you're finished.
(Observe children and give feedback.)
- Everybody, does rat 3 make a **left** turn or a **right** turn? (Signal.) *A right turn.*

7. Touch the picture that shows rat 4. ✔
Turn your page so that rat 4 is facing straight up.
(Observe children and give feedback.)
- Now write **R** on the rat's **right** front paw. Then write **R** or **L** in the circle to show if the rat turns **right** or **left.** Think big. And don't get fooled. Raise your hand when you're finished.
(Observe children and give feedback.)
- Everybody, does rat 4 make a **left** turn or a **right** turn? (Signal.) *A left turn.*

8. Raise your hand if you wrote the correct letter for all four circles. ✔
Wow, you didn't get fooled on left and right.

Teaching Notes

The biggest problem the children have is orienting the page so the rat is facing straight up. (In this example, the numbers on the rat are right-side-up when the rat is facing straight up.)

Observe children carefully in all the steps that require children to rotate their workbook page.

If some children have trouble on more than one step, show them how to orient the page; then return the page to the original position and tell them: "Now you do it. Turn the page so the rat is facing straight up."

Later maze problems involve testing assertions the Bragging Rats make about mazes. In lesson 48, one of the Bragging Rats says that he got out of a maze by just taking right turns. Children test this assertion by seeing if it is possible to get out of the maze by taking only right turns. After they show you the route, they pencil it in.

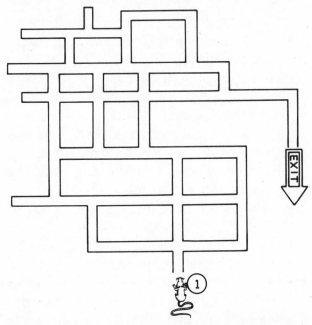

Children also apply right and left to rotating objects. In lesson 49, they are shown that turning a screw works just like turning right or left in a maze.

(**Note:** Children are prompted to look at how the top of the screw turns, not the bottom. Sometimes children have great trouble following the directions, "Turn the screw to the right," because they do not understand that the directions tell how the top of the screw turns.)

Questions and Clues

Questions and Clues are used as a kind of classification game that relates to binary-logic activities. The general format for Questions and Clues involves starting with a set of objects and using information from a "clue" to eliminate some objects. The procedure is repeated until all but one object is eliminated and children have discovered the mystery object.

After children have learned the general format of using clues, they generate questions for finding the "mystery picture." The objective for many activities is to find the mystery picture by asking only three questions. These activities shape children's strategy for generating "smart" questions, those that will systematically eliminate possibilities.

The first "clue" activity is introduced in lesson 25. Here's part of the introduction.

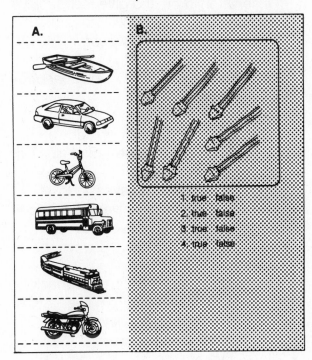

5. You're going to play a mystery game. It's a very hard game. Here's how it works: I'll tell you clues about the mystery vehicle. After each clue, you'll be able to fold over some pictures that could **not** be the mystery vehicle. After I give you the last clue, you'll know which vehicle is the mystery vehicle because it will be the **only** picture that is **not** folded over. Does that game sound pretty tough?

6. Here's the first clue about the mystery vehicle: This vehicle has wheels. Everybody, say that clue. (Signal.) *This vehicle has wheels.*

• Not all the vehicles have wheels. If it does **not** have wheels, it can **not** be the mystery vehicle. So fold over any vehicle that does **not** have wheels. Just turn it over the way you would turn a page in a book. Raise your hand when you're finished.
(Observe children and give feedback.)

• Everybody, which vehicle did you fold over? (Signal.) *The rowboat.*

• Why did you fold over the rowboat? (Call on a child. Idea: *A rowboat does not have wheels.*)

7. Here's another clue about the mystery vehicle: This vehicle has windows. Everybody, say that clue. (Signal.) *This vehicle has windows.*

• Listen: If it does **not** have windows, it can **not** be the mystery vehicle, so fold over any vehicle that does **not** have windows. Raise your hand when you're finished.
(Observe children and give feedback.)

• Which vehicles did you fold over? (Call on a child. Idea: *The bicycle and motorcycle.*)

• Why did you fold over the bicycle and motorcycle? (Call on a child. Idea: *A bicycle and a motorcycle do not have windows.*)

8. Here's another clue about the mystery vehicle: This vehicle can hold **more** than ten people. Everybody, say that clue. (Signal.) *This vehicle can hold more than ten people.*

• Listen: If it can **not** hold more than ten people, it can **not** be the mystery vehicle, so fold over any vehicle that can **not** hold more than ten people. Raise your hand when you're finished. (Observe children and give feedback.)

• Everybody, which vehicle did you fold over? (Signal.) *The car.*

• Why did you fold over the car? (Call on a child. Idea: *A car cannot hold more than ten people.*)

9. Here's the last clue about the mystery vehicle: This vehicle runs on tracks. Everybody, say that clue. (Signal.) *This vehicle runs on tracks.*

• Listen: Fold over the picture that could **not** be the mystery vehicle. ✔

• Everybody, which vehicle did you fold over? (Signal.) *The bus.*

• Why did you fold over the bus? (Call on a child. Idea: *A bus does not run on tracks.*)

10. You figured out which vehicle is the mystery vehicle. It should be the **only** picture that is **not** folded over. Everybody, which vehicle is the mystery vehicle? (Signal.) *The train.*

• Raise your hand if you figured out the mystery vehicle. ✔

11. I gave you four clues that let you figure out the mystery vehicle. Let's see how many of those clues you remember.

• What was one of the clues? (Call on a child. Accept appropriate response.)

12. What was another clue? (Call on a child. Accept appropriate response.) (Repeat step 12 until all clues have been identified.)

13. Who can name all four clues about the mystery vehicle? (Call on several children. Praise any child who can name at least three clues.)

14. You did such a good job on the mystery game that we'll play it again next time.

In the steps not shown here, children identify the objects and the class, and they cut "flaps" (cut along the dotted lines).

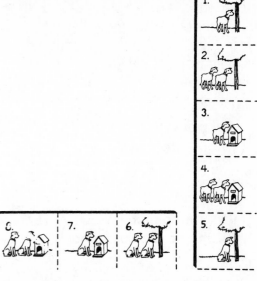

In some later lessons, children play a variation of the game by making an **X** through each object that cannot be the mystery picture. Beginning with lesson 62, children use the glossary at the back of their workbook to play "mystery" games.

Exercises that require children to generate questions about the mystery picture begin in lesson 37. In this activity, you prompt the kind of questions they should ask. Beginning in lesson 43, you divide the class into 4 teams. Children work cooperatively. (See Organization, page 20, for more about teams.) Each team develops three questions that will lead to the identification of the mystery object.

Children first cut the flaps. Here's the part of the exercise that follows.

3. Now, let's play the toughest game of all. We'll see which teams can do it. Remember, if you're **really** smart, your team can find the mystery picture by asking only **three** questions. But they have to be **super** questions. You're working in teams. So your team has to agree on each question before the team asks it. Everybody on a team figures out which questions your team will ask. When your team has your first question, raise your hands and I'll come over. You'll whisper the question to me so that none of the other teams can hear the question. I'll whisper the answer, and you'll fold over the pictures that could **not** be the mystery picture.

4. (**Key:** The target picture is 7—one dog sitting next to a doghouse.)

- You know your **first** question is good if you can fold over **four** pictures after I answer your first question. Remember, you're trying to find the mystery picture in only **three** questions. Raise your hands when your team has a good question.

> **Answers**:
> *(How many dogs?)* One.
> *(What is the dog doing?)* Sitting.
> *(Where is the dog?)* Next to a doghouse.
> (Do **not** combine answers, such as: **Sitting next to** a doghouse.)

5. (After you answer each team's question, tell the team to fold over the pictures that could **not** be the mystery picture. Then ask them if that was a good question. Remind them by saying:) For a good first question, you can fold over four pictures.
- (Then direct each team to agree on the next question. Tell them:) If it's a good question, you can fold over two pictures.
- (Repeat the procedure for the third question:) If it's a good question, you'll know which picture is the mystery picture.
6. (After any team has found the mystery picture by asking only three questions, tell the class:) We have a winner. We have a team that found the mystery picture by asking only **three** questions.
- (Call on a team member to say the three questions. Do not accept "combined" questions.)
7. Everybody, what's the number of the mystery picture? (Signal.) *Seven.*
- How many dogs are in that picture? (Signal.) *One.*
- What is the dog doing? (Signal.) *Sitting.*
- Where is the dog? (Signal.) *Next to a doghouse.*

Teaching Notes

Do not accept combined questions (2 questions), such as, "Are there two dogs and are they standing?" Questions like, "Are two dogs standing next to the doghouse?" are not acceptable. They are often not good questions. (If the answer is "yes," you know the picture. If the answer is "no," you have learned very little.)

When you answer questions, make sure that you do not give additional information. If children ask, "Where are the dogs?" for their first question, don't reject the question or indicate that there's only one dog. Just say, "I'll tell you where. Next to the doghouse." Do not say, "Sitting next to the doghouse."

Similarly, if children ask, "What are the dogs doing?" just say, "Sitting." Don't say, "Sitting next to the doghouse."

In earlier lessons, children learned the rule that, if their first question is good, they should be able to turn over half the pictures (in this case, four pictures). Use this rule when giving feedback on the first question. "If you can't turn over four pictures, that was not a very good question."

When children work cooperatively, praise teams that have their three questions formulated quickly. Let the other teams know that this behavior is desirable. "Team C already has its questions. That's really working together well."

Also praise groups for working quietly. "I can't hear the things that team B is saying. They're working hard, but none of the other groups can hear them."

Variations of the question-generating activities are used to ask about specific objects in the glossary. For these questions, children may refer to columns, groups of columns, class names and features of objects. (Questions such as, "Is it in the first or second column?" are acceptable.)

Data

In some lessons, children summarize data. They write data in tables that are similar to tables used in math projects. The focus of data collection in Level A is on the "truth" of statements that characters make about different data-generating situations.

Here's the first part of the exercise from lesson 42 and the children's workbook page.

1. You've heard a story about a woman named Bonnie who bought a birdbath for her yard.

> One day, Bonnie was talking to her neighbors. Bonnie said, "I always have red birds and yellow birds and blue birds in my yard. But there are always more **red** birds than any other color."
>
> One neighbor said, "No, that's not true. I've looked in your yard many times when I was trying to find Sweetie. And I know for a fact that there are always more **yellow** birds than any other color."
>
> "Not true," another neighbor said. "Every time I've looked in your yard while walking my wonderful dog, Honey, I've always seen more **blue** birds than birds of any other color."

- If the wise old rat heard this conversation, how do you think he'd go about finding the right answer? (Call on a child. Idea: *Count the birds.*)
- Yes, the smart way is to find out the answer by counting the birds. So **you** can be smart.

2. Look at the picture for part D. The letters on the birds show what color they should be. The letter **R** on a bird shows that the bird should be **red.**

- Your turn: Take out your **red** crayon and put a **red** mark on all the birds that have the letter **R** on them. Don't miss any birds, but do it fast and don't color the whole bird. Just put a red mark on each bird inside the picture that has an **R** on it. Don't color the bird in the big box. Raise your hand when you're finished.
(Observe children and give feedback.)

3. Now look at the box below the picture. You'll see a picture of a bird with an **R** on it.

- Touch that bird. ✔
  Right after that bird are the words **red birds.** Then there's an empty box. Write the number of **red** birds in that box. Count all the red birds in the picture and write that number in the top box. Raise your hand when you're finished.
  (Observe children and give feedback.)
- Everybody, what number did you write for the **red** birds? **(Signal.)** *Ten.*
4. Now do the same thing for the **yellow** birds. Make a **yellow** mark on every bird in the picture that has the letter **Y** on it. The **Y** is for **yellow.** After you make your yellow marks, count the **yellow** birds and write that number in the box for **yellow** birds. Raise your hand when you're finished.
  (Observe children and give feedback.)
- Everybody, what number did you write for the **yellow** birds? **(Signal.)** *Six.*
5. Now do the same thing for the **blue** birds. Make a **blue** mark on every bird in the picture that has the letter **B** on it. The **B** is for **blue.** After you make your blue marks, count the **blue** birds and write that number in the box for **blue** birds. Raise your hand when you're finished.
  (Observe children and give feedback.)
- Everybody, what number did you write? **(Signal.)** *Seven.*
6. Get ready to read your numbers one more time.
- Listen: How many **red** birds are in the picture? **(Signal.)** *Ten.*
- How many **yellow** birds are in the picture? **(Signal.)** *Six.*
- How many **blue** birds are in the picture? **(Signal.)** *Seven.*
7. Let's see who was right about the birds in Bonnie's yard. Here's what Bonnie said: "There are always more **red** birds than any other color."
- Think about it. Is that statement true or false? **(Signal.)** *True.*

- One neighbor said, "There are always more **yellow** birds than any other color." Is that statement true or false? **(Signal.)** *False.*
- Another neighbor said that there are always more **blue** birds than any other color. Is that statement true or false? **(Signal.)** *False.*
- So who was right, Bonnie or one of her neighbors? **(Signal.)** *Bonnie.*
8. Before we leave this picture, there's one more box to fill out below the picture, but I really don't know what goes in there.
- Touch the last box below the picture. ✔ It says, **other animals.** I guess they want you to write the number of other animals that are in the picture. But I really don't see any. Maybe you do. Look at the picture very carefully. See if you can find any other animals in the picture. Count up any animals that are **not** birds and write that number in the last box. If you don't find any other animals, you can write **zero** in the box. Raise your hand when you have a number in the last box.
  (Observe children and give feedback.)
- Everybody, what number did you write for **other animals?** **(Signal.)** *Two.*
- I guess they were hiding in the picture. I didn't see them.
9. Later, you can color everything in part D.

Children mark each bird with its appropriate color (red for R, yellow for Y and blue for B). Then they count the number of each type of bird and write the number in the "table" at the bottom of the page.

For one of the later data-collection problems, children count the number of left turns and right turns a rat takes to get out of a maze.

Alternative Solutions

Beginning in lesson 41, children work problems that have more than one solution. These activities integrate what children have learned about true/false and about all-some-none.

In lesson 41, children identify the statement that is true about the cats: **None of the cats have a tail.** They make the statement false by drawing tails. Possibly they make tails on all the cats. Possibly they make tails on only some of the cats.

- I'll say some statements about the cats. You listen. Then tell me the statement that is true.

2. Listen: **All** of the cats have a tail. **None** of the cats have a tail. **Some** of the cats have a tail.

- Your turn: Say the statement that's **true** about the cats. (Signal.) *None of the cats have a tail.*

3. Listen: Make that statement **false** by drawing something in your picture. When you fix up the picture the right way, a **different** statement will be true about the picture. You won't be able to say: **None** of the cats have a tail. But you'll be able to say something else about the cats and their tails. Maybe you'll be able to say: **Some** of the cats have a tail. Maybe you'll be able to say: **All** of the cats have a tail. Fix up the picture. Raise your hand when you're finished.

(Observe children and give feedback.)

- Listen: Raise your hand if you made a tail on **all** of the cats. ✔
- Listen: Raise your hand if you made a tail on **some** of the cats. ✔
  Either of those ways will work.

4. Look at your cats again. **None** of the cats have a tail. True or false? (Signal.) *False.*

- (Call on a child:) Make a statement that is true about **your** cats.
  (After child responds, say:) Hold up your book so everybody can see if your statement is true.

- Who can make a **different** statement that's true about **their** cats? (Call on a child. After child responds, say:) Hold up your book so everybody can see if your statement is true.

- Yes, two statements could be true about the cats. **Some** of the cats have a tail *or all* of the cats have a tail.

5. Wow, that was tough and you did a great job.

Different variations of this activity are presented through lesson 53.

Story Grammar

The stories presented in Level A are the heart of the program. Concepts that have been taught are incorporated in the stories. The different story grammars acquaint children with various patterns for anticipating and predicting outcomes.

The pattern for the story exercises is for the story to be presented two or three times. With each reading of the story, a different workbook activity is presented. After the introduction of the story, children encounter new stories or activities involving familiar characters and familiar story grammars.

Here's a list of the stories and the lesson in which each story is presented.

During the introduction of a story, you ask specified questions. Later, when you reread a story, fewer questions are presented.

Here's the introduction of the story *Sweetie and the Birdbath* (lesson 3). The text of the story is in the ruled box.

1. Everybody, I'm going to read you a story. Listen to the things that happen in the story because you're going to have to fix up a picture that shows part of the story.

2. This is a story about a mean cat named Sweetie and the adventure he had with a birdbath. The story starts before there was a birdbath. Listen:

> A woman named Bonnie loved birds. One day she noticed some birds cleaning themselves by splashing in a puddle on the sidewalk. She said, "Those birds shouldn't have to splash in a puddle to get clean. They need a birdbath." That was a good idea.

- Listen: What did Bonnie see that gave her the idea that the birds needed a birdbath? (Call on a child. Idea: *Bonnie saw the birds splashing in a puddle.*)

> The more Bonnie thought about getting a birdbath the more she liked the idea. "I will get a birdbath big enough for all the birds that want to take a bath."
> So Bonnie went to the pet store and looked at birdbaths. She picked out the biggest birdbath they had.

- Listen: Where did Bonnie go to get a birdbath? (Call on a child.) *To the pet store.*
- Which birdbath did she pick out? (Call on a child. Idea: *The biggest one they had.*)

> The next day, a truck delivered the birdbath. Bonnie set it up in her backyard and soon some birds saw it. They called to their friends and the first thing you know all kinds of birds were splashing in the birdbath—red birds, yellow birds, spotted birds and little brown birds.

- See if you can get a picture in your mind of that birdbath with lots of birds in it.

- What color are the birds in the birdbath? (Call on a child. Idea: *Red, yellow, brown and spotted.*)
- What are those birds doing? (Call on a child. Idea: *Splashing in the birdbath.*)

Following the story-reading is a workbook activity with an illustration of part of the story. Here's the picture and activities following the introduction of the Sweetie story.

D.

- Everybody, find the picture of Sweetie. That's part D. ✔
  Here's a picture of something that happened in the story.
- What's Sweetie doing in this picture? (Call on a child. Idea: *Grabbing the eagle.*)
- Everybody, is Sweetie all wet yet? (Signal.) *No.*
- What's going to happen right **after** this picture is over? (Call on a child. Idea: *Sweetie will get slammed into the birdbath.*)
- Everybody, does that eagle look happy? (Signal.) *No.*

- Look in the trees.
  There are 10 birds in the trees. See if you can find all of them and color them the right colors. Who remembers what colors they are? (Call on a child. Idea: *Red, yellow, brown and spotted.*)
- Color the birds.
  Then color the rest of the picture.
- Everybody, what color is Sweetie? (Signal.) *Yellow.*
- That eagle is brown and white. The brown parts are a little darker, but they are not brown. You'll have to color them brown.

The *Sweetie and the Birdbath* story is reread in several other lessons. Each lesson has a new workbook activity that involves some part of the story. The purpose of the re-readings of each story is to thoroughly acquaint children with details of each story grammar.

For the major story characters, extensions or extrapolations follow the original story. Some new story extensions involve familiar characters and the same basic story grammar as the original story.

EXTENDING STORY GRAMMARS
The first extension story appears in lesson 11. The story involves a character named Paul who, in an earlier story, painted things purple. When paint dripped on something near where Paul was painting, he solved the problem by painting it purple. Here's the extension activity from lesson 11.

To tell the story, children follow the basic story grammar. For example, "When Paul is painting the piggy bank, some paint flew over and landed on the pillow. He said, 'That looks bad, but I know how to fix it,' and he did. He painted the whole pillow pink . . . ."

The illustrations for extensions are designed so that they have lots of hidden features. In this picture, for instance, many things that aren't labeled are p-starting words. In the picture are palm trees, pyramids, polka dots, a poodle with paws and a parrot on a perch. You may decide to point out some of these objects to the children.

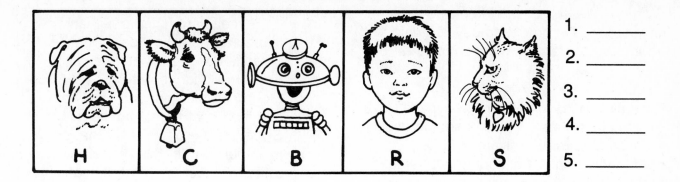

1. _____
2. _____
3. _____
4. _____
5. _____

CHARACTER IDENTIFICATION

Some extrapolation activities involve identifying characters by what they say. Here's part of an activity from lesson 45. (Before this part of the exercise, children have identified the pictures and the first letter of each character's name.)

8. Everybody, touch number 1 and keep touching it. ✔
   - Listen and don't say anything. Here's the statement for number 1: "I'd love to go roller-skating just like those children are doing."
   - Find the character who would say that. Write the letter for that character on line 1. Raise your hand when you're finished.
   (Observe children and give feedback.)

9. Everybody, which character would love to go roller-skating just like the children? (Signal.) *Clarabelle.*
   - So what letter did you write for number 1? (Signal.) *C.*
   - (Write on the board:)

   1. C_____

   - Here's what you should have for number 1. Raise your hand if you got it right. ✔

10. Everybody, touch number 2. ✔ Listen and don't say anything. Here's the statement for number 2: "Look at those little chicks. Yum, yum."
    - Find the character who would say that. Write the letter for that character on line 2. Raise your hand when you're finished.
    (Observe children and give feedback.)

11. Everybody, which character would say, "Look at those little chicks. Yum, yum"? (Signal.) *Sweetie.*
    - So what letter did you write for number 2? (Signal.) *S.*
    - (Write to show:)

    1. C_____
    2. S_____

    - Here's what you should have for number 2. Raise your hand if you got it right. ✔

12. Everybody, touch number 3. ✔
    - Listen and don't say anything. Here's the statement for number 3: "When I sat down, my hat was right over there; but now, I don't know where it is."
    - Find the character who would say that. Write the letter for that character on line 3. Raise your hand when you're finished.
    (Observe children and give feedback.)

13. Everybody, which character would have trouble finding a hat? (Signal.) *Roger.*
    - So what letter did you write for number 3? (Signal.) *R.*
    - (Write to show:)

    1. C_____
    2. S_____
    3. R_____

    - Here's what you should have for number 3. Raise your hand if you got it right. ✔

Starting in lesson 55, children also work cooperatively in groups to develop unique utterances for familiar story characters.

STORY COMPLETION/PLAY

Beginning in lesson 55, children make up endings to stories that are based on familiar story grammars. For these activities, you read the first part of a story about Sweetie and the mirror. Sweetie, who had never encountered a mirror that went all the way down to the floor, was in a place where he saw such a mirror, but he didn't know it was a mirror. He challenged the cat in the mirror. Every time he moved, the cat in the mirror moved. Here's the story-completion activity and the play that follows.

> Sweetie said to himself, "That cat is ugly, but it has to be the **fastest** cat I ever saw. When I do something, it seems to do the same thing at the same time I do it."
> Then Sweetie said to himself, "It's time to teach this cat a lesson." So he crouched down, leaped at the yellow cat and . . .

2. That's all there is to the story. We're going to have to make up the ending ourselves. Remember, Sweetie gets fooled and then he always says something at the end of these stories.
   • Here's where the story stops: Sweetie crouched down, leaped at the yellow cat and . . .
   • Now think of what happened to fool Sweetie. Tell what happened when Sweetie jumped. Then tell what Sweetie **thought** happened and what Sweetie said at the end of the story. (Call on several children. Praise ideas such as: *Sweetie bonked himself on the mirror. Then Sweetie said something like, "That yellow cat may be ugly, but he sure can hit hard and fast."*
3. So here's an ending to the story. See if this is a good one.

> Sweetie crouched down and leaped at the yellow cat. Bonk. Sweetie banged his head against the mirror and went flying. He rolled around on the floor and finally sat up and looked at the cat in the mirror. Sweetie said to himself, "That sure is an ugly cat, but let me tell you, that cat is fast and that cat can really hit hard."

EXERCISE 5

PUTTING ON A PLAY
Sweetie and the Mirror

1. Let's see if we have two children who can act out that story about Sweetie. One child will play Sweetie. The other child will play the cat in the mirror.
   • (Call on two children. Tell one:) You're Sweetie.
   (Tell the other:) You're the cat in the mirror.
   (Have children face each other about 10 feet apart.)
2. Okay, I'll tell each part of the story. Then I'll tell our cats to act out that part.

> Sweetie saw the cat in the mirror. Sweetie arched his back. And the cat in the mirror did the same thing.

• Go cats. ✔

> Next Sweetie made the meanest face he could make. And the cat in the mirror did the same thing.

• Go cats. ✔

> Next Sweetie crouched down and moved toward the yellow cat, closer, closer, closer and the cat in the mirror did the same thing.

- Go cats. ✔

> Now Sweetie held up his **left** paw and showed his claws. And the cat in the mirror held up its **right** paw, the same way.

- Remember, Sweetie, your **left** paw. Cats go. ✔

> Next Sweetie crouched down and leaped at the yellow cat and went sprawling.

- Cats, be careful and don't **really** bang into each other. Go. ✔

> Now Sweetie is completely fooled by the mirror and he says something to himself.

- Say it, Sweetie. (Idea: *"That sure is an ugly-looking cat, but let me tell you, that cat is fast and that cat can really hit hard."*)
3. That was pretty good. Maybe next time, we can do it again with a different Sweetie and a different cat in the mirror.

Teaching Notes

This story involves the relative notion of left and right. Sweetie holds up his left paw. The cat in the mirror holds up his right. By lesson 45, children have been taught this relationship.

The activities presented in the Story-Grammar track are designed to shape children's understanding in a way that will serve them later in both reading and writing. The major presentation required to make the activities work well is to read the stories in a manner that makes them sound interesting. If you provide good reading and follow the activities, children will learn a lot about story-grammar activities.

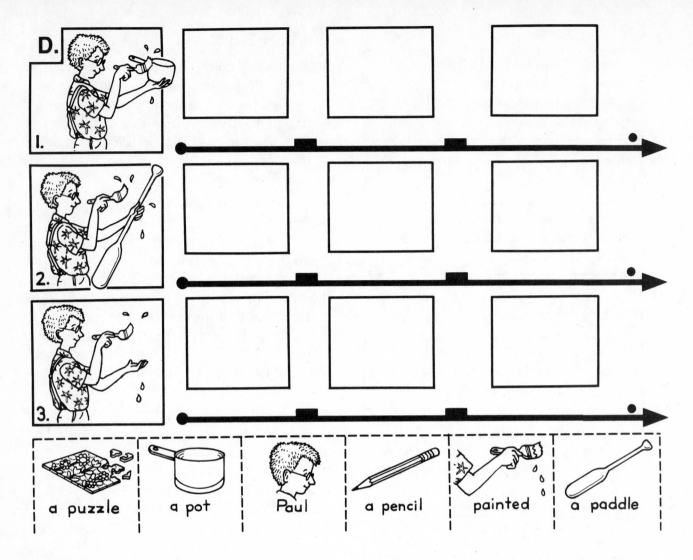

Writing

Throughout the Following-Directions activities and in the other tracks, children write symbols, copy letters and copy words. Most of the writing activities involve creating sentences.

The Sentence-Writing activities are not introduced until after lesson 50 because the children typically have not learned enough about writing or reading to handle writing tasks earlier in the program.

The Writing activities show children the relationship between words and specific "ideas." Before children write, they construct word-picture sentences for different illustrations. Here's an example from lesson 53.

The pictures show what Paul did. You're going to make up sentences that tell what he did.

2. Look at the cut-outs at the bottom of the page. There are words at the bottom of each cut-out. I'll read the words.
- Touch the first cut-out. ✔
  The words say: **a puzzle.**
- Touch the next cut-out. ✔
  The words say: **a pot.**
- Touch the next cut-out. ✔
  The word says: **Paul.**
- Touch the next cut-out. ✔
  The words say: **a pencil.**
- Touch the next cut-out. ✔
  The word says: **painted.**
- Touch the last cut-out. ✔
  The words say: **a paddle.**

3. Your turn: Cut out the pictures at the bottom of the page along the dotted lines. Raise your hand when you have all your cut-outs ready.
(Observe children and give feedback.)

4. Everybody, touch picture 1. ✔
That picture shows something Paul did. What did he do in that picture? (Signal.) *Painted a pot.*

- Here's the sentence that tells what Paul did: **Paul painted a pot.**

5. Everybody, say that sentence. (Signal.) *Paul painted a pot.*
(Repeat step 5 until firm.)

6. (Write on the board:)

- You're going to use your cut-out pictures to show that sentence. Here's how you'll do it: You'll put the cut-outs for picture 1 in the three boxes next to picture 1.

- (Write **Paul painted** in the first and second boxes on the board:)

- Listen: **Paul painted** a pot.
- (Touch the first box.)
So you put the cut-out for **Paul** here.
- (Touch the second box.)
Then you put the cut-out for **painted** here.
- Do that much. Put the cut-outs for **Paul** and **painted** in the first two boxes. The words are on the cut-outs. Raise your hand when you're finished.
(Observe children and give feedback.)

7. Everybody, touch picture 1 again. ✔
Say the whole sentence for that picture. (Signal.) *Paul painted a pot.*

- Fix up the cut-outs by putting the right cut-out in the last box. Remember, you want your cut-outs to say: **Paul painted a pot.** Raise your hand when you're finished.
(Observe children and give feedback.)
- Everybody, what picture did you put in the last box? (Signal.) *A pot.*
- (Write to show:)

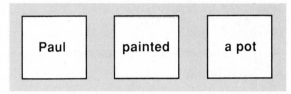

- Here's what the words in your boxes should say. Raise your hand if you got it right. ✔

The activity requires children to express a single picture as a series of segmented ideas, each expressed by a word unit. Picture 1 shows Paul painting a pot. To express the idea, the children first name Paul, then indicate what he did.

The worksheet picture doesn't show what Paul painted in the last picture. After children have completed sentences for the first two pictures and copied the sentences on the arrow below each row of cut-outs, they have an opportunity to make a sentence for the last picture.

Here's the script:

12. Oh, dear. There's another picture of Paul on the page, but the picture doesn't show what Paul painted. Maybe you could make up a sentence about what Paul did by using your cut-outs.

- Put your cut-outs in the boxes for picture 3 so you make up a sentence that tells about something else Paul did. Don't make up one of the sentences you've already written. Raise your hand when you're finished.
(Observe children and give feedback.)

- (Call on several children:) Read the sentence you made up about Paul. (Praise appropriate sentences.)

13. Everybody, touch the **arrow** for picture 3. ✔
    Listen: Copy the sentence you made up for picture 3. Raise your hand when you're finished.
    (Observe children and give feedback.)

14. Everybody, turn your cut-outs over and put them in a pile. Let's see who can read all three of their sentences. (Call on several children. Praise correct responses.)

In later lessons, a variation of the same procedure is used, except that the children do not cut out the pictures and put them in place. Instead, they go over the words, say the sentences for pictures and write the sentences (copying the words from the appropriate boxes).

Here's the workbook page from lesson 61 and the last part of the teacher-directed activity. The children have already written their sentences for the first two illustrations.

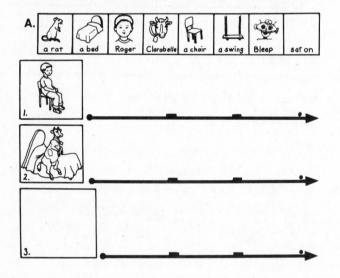

9. There is no picture 3. So here's what you'll do: First you'll make up a sentence that tells what the picture will show. You can write a sentence that uses any of the characters in the boxes. But don't write a sentence we've already done. Write your sentence. Raise your hand when you're finished.
   (Observe children and give feedback.)

10. I'm going to call on several children to read their sentence for picture 3.
    - (Call on a child to read sentence 3. Repeat with several children.)
      (Praise original sentences that take the form: *(Name) sat on _____.*)

11. Let's make sure you can read all of your sentences.
    - (Call on several children:) Read all three sentences you wrote.
      (Praise children who read appropriate sentences in correct order.)

12. Later, you'll have to draw a picture for sentence 3. Remember, your picture will show what your sentence says.
    - (Call on several children:) What will your picture show?
      (Praise those children whose response tells about their sentence.)

13. I'll show you some of the better pictures later.

Starting in lesson 68, children cooperatively write endings to stories. Children listen to the first part of a story involving Clarabelle: Sixteen frogs were on a log that was floating near the shore of a lake. The frogs were sitting and sunning. Clarabelle saw them and said to herself, "My, that looks like fun. I would love to sit on that log." When she tiptoed into the water, the frogs told her, "Get out of here. Can't you see that this is a frog log, not a cow log?" But when Clarabelle . . . .

After children tell their ending to the story, they dictate an ending to the story, which you write on the board. Then children copy the ending.

Lesson 70 provides a model for extending writing assignments beyond the 70 lessons of Level A.

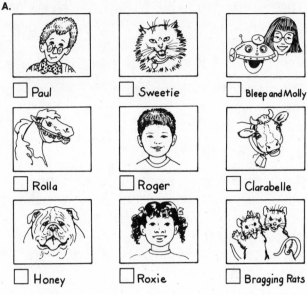

A.

☐ Paul   ☐ Sweetie   ☐ Bleep and Molly

☐ Rolla   ☐ Roger   ☐ Clarabelle

☐ Honey   ☐ Roxie   ☐ Bragging Rats

1. We don't have any more lessons in this program. But we need some more stories for our library, so you're going to write them.
- First we have to figure out which characters we're going to write about.
2. Everybody, find part A. ✔
Those are pictures of the characters you've read about. You have to pick your three favorite characters. Those are the characters you'd like to write about most.
- Here's how you do that: You make a check in the box by your three favorite characters. Remember, you can make only three check marks. So look over the characters carefully. Select the three you'd like to write about most and put check marks for those three characters. Remember, only three characters. Do it now.
(Observe children and give feedback.)

3. Let's see who the all-time favorites are. (Write on the board:)

Paul

- Raise your hand if you made a check for Paul. ✔
(Count children's raised hands. Write the number after Paul.)
- (Repeat step 3 for the rest of the characters:)

Paul ☐
Sweetie ☐
Bleep and Molly ☐
Rolla ☐
Roger ☐
Clarabelle ☐
Honey ☐
Roxie ☐
Bragging Rats ☐

4. (Announce the three winning characters.)
5. (Assign children to four teams.)
We'll work in teams to make up one good story today. Each team should get together and decide which of the three characters they want to tell about today.
- Talk to your teammates and agree on one of the three winning characters. Raise your hands when you're finished. ✔
- (Ask each team which character they want to tell about.)

6. Now each team is going to work together to make up a good story about the character you chose. Remember, the stories you make up must be the right kind of story for the character. So work out the details. Then each team will tell their story to me. I'll write it. We'll see if each team can come up with a great story. (Observe teams and give feedback. Praise teams that consider different ideas. Praise cute ideas.)

7. (Direct each team to dictate a story. Write it on the board or on a piece of paper to be duplicated.)

• (For later assignments:
   a) teams can make up a story for one of the other characters;
   b) children can individually copy and illustrate one or more of the stories;
   c) teams can make up a story based on a made-up character not introduced in the program.)

Similar activities can be developed for other writing. It's a good idea to assign children to make up stories about the characters in Level A, and not simply write other stories, to assure that they follow the story grammar for each character.

Tests

In-program Tests

The in-program tests that appear as every tenth lesson of the program provide a basis for periodically judging the progress of individual children and for awarding grades.

During a test, children should be seated so they cannot "copy."

Directions for presenting the test appear as part of each test lesson.

When observing children's performance, make sure that they are following directions, but do not tell them answers to any item or give them "hints." (The answer key for each test appears in Exercise 3 of each test lesson.)

Collect student workbooks and mark the tests. If children do poorly on a test, check their work on preceding lessons to determine whether children had problems with the tested concepts when they were presented earlier in the program. Also note discrepancies. If a child does poorly on a test, but very well on all preceding exercises, the child may have been copying.

Mark each item a child misses on the test. Use the answer key as the guide. Any deviations are mistakes.

Count the number of mistakes and enter the number at the top of each child's test. If the child missed three items, the score is −3.

Before returning the test forms, use your copy of the Reproducible Group Summary Sheet that appears on page 92 and enter the number of errors each child made.

If you are developing skills profiles based on each child's progress, reproduce the summary on pages 87–91 for each child and circle the appropriate score.

Test Remedies

Test remedies are appropriate for children who miss test items. It is possible to use formulas for administering test remedies (if 30% of the children miss an item, present the remedy); however, the goal of the remedies would be to fix up each child's misunderstanding. Children who make more than one mistake on any part of the test should receive a remedy for that part. One procedure for doing this is to:

1. Repeat an exercise in the program (from the preceding 9 lessons) that deals with the difficult skill.
2. Then present the test again or the part of the test on which children had trouble.

Below is a list of exercises of the program that should be repeated for the various parts of the tests. Although the workbook is copyrighted and may not normally be reproduced, you may reproduce the parts of the workbook needed for test remedies. After firming children on the remedies, repeat the test or the part of the test the children failed.

Test	Test part failed	For remedy, present:		
		Presentation Book Exercise	Lesson	Workbook Part
1	A	2	9	A
	B	3	6	B
	C	3	9	B
2	A	1	18	A
	B	2	19	A
	C	4	19	C
	D	3	19	B
3	A	2	28	B
	B	1	29	A
	C	3	28	C
4	A	4	39	D
	B	4	35	D
	C	3	39	C
5	A	4	44	C
	B	4	45	D
6	A	1	59	A
	B	2	59	B
	C	3	59	C

Objectives

The objectives on pages 81 to 86 show the development of skills and applications taught in *Reasoning and Writing, Level A.*

The skills and applications are grouped by tracks. The headings indicate the major tracks and the divisions within each track. Each track shows the development of a major topic, such as Story Grammar or Classification. Typically, a track will have activities that are presented over many different lessons of the program.

The major tracks are

> FOLLOWING DIRECTIONS
> TRUE/FALSE
> SEQUENCING
> IF-THEN
> ALL, SOME, NONE
> CLASSIFICATION
> RIGHT/LEFT
> QUESTIONS AND CLUES
> DATA
> ALTERNATIVE SOLUTIONS
> STORY GRAMMAR
> WRITING

There are divisions within some tracks. Each division is marked by a subheading.

The subheadings for Classification are

> GROUPS
> BINARY LOGIC

The subheadings for Questions and Clues are

> USING
> GENERATING

The subheadings for Story Grammar are

> MODEL STORIES
> APPLICATION
> EXTRAPOLATION
> PLAYS

Although the objectives show the various categories and the lessons in which each specific objective is taught, the objectives do not show the interrelationships among the various skills. Specific skills are involved in more than one track. For instance, children learn to make statements that are **true** and statements that are **false** about pictures. Some of the statements require children to refer to **all,** or **some,** or **none.** For example, children will start with a picture that shows some of the balloons with a string. Children fix up the picture so that all of the balloons have a string. Children then make two true statements: one about the picture before they changed it (**Some of the balloons had a string**) and one about the picture after they changed it (**All the balloons have a string**). This activity is listed under the True/False track; however, it also involves **all, some,** and **none,** which is another major track. Children also use the concepts of **all, some, none** in the track, Alternative Solutions. For activities in this track, children identify alternative solutions for making an **all** or **some** statement true. For instance, children are presented with a picture that shows **None of the cats have a tail.** Children fix up the picture to make that statement false. The result is a picture that shows **All of the cats have a tail,** or **Some of the cats have a tail.**

Similarly, the Story Grammar track relates to nearly all the other tracks in the program. Specific stories, applications and extrapolations of basic story grammar involve tasks that require knowledge of all some-none, true/false, right/left, alternative solutions, data, classification, sequencing and so forth.

In summary, the objectives show the various skills and applications that are taught; however, skills and applications developed in one track invariably spill over into other tracks as children use and apply what they have learned.

Following Directions	Objectives	Lessons
	Follow directions involving plural words and singular words.	1, 2
	Follow directions for marking specified symbols with check marks.	1, 2
	Follow directions involving position words and plurals.	3, 4
	Follow directions for marking symbols with specified colors.	3, 4
	Follow directions involving position words and the word **not**.	5
	Follow directions for marking symbols.	5, 6
	Follow directions involving the words **and** and **not**.	6–9
	Follow directions involving **or**.	13, 14
	Follow directions involving **same**.	14
	Follow directions involving **right** and **left**.	25–27, 38

True/False		
	Circle pictures to indicate which actions an animal can do or can't do.	1
	Circle the word **true** or **false** for pictures to indicate which actions an animal or person can do (**true**) or can't do (**false**).	2–9, 11
	Circle the word **true** or **false** for statements.	12, 13
	Identify the pictures for true statements involving **all, some** and **none**.	14
	Say true statements and false statements for pictures showing **all, some,** and **none**.	15, 16
	Fix up pictures to show true statements involving **all**.	18, 19
	Fix up pictures to show true statements involving **some**.	21–24
	Fix up a picture to show true statements involving **all** and **some**.	25–27, 31, 35, 36, 45
	Construct true statements about a picture that has been changed.	28, 32–34, 38, 44, 51
	Fix up a picture to show false statements involving **all** and **some**.	37, 39

Sequencing

Objectives	Lessons
Perform a sequence of actions based on a series of pictures.	1–4
Number pictures to correspond to a demonstrated series of actions.	5, 6, 11
Relate a sequence of actions to a picture with numbers (1, 2, 3, 4) showing where the various actions occurred.	7, 8
Relate a familiar story to a picture that has numbers showing where the various events occurred.	9, 24
Write numbers to show a sequence of events and tell a story based on familiar story grammar.	13, 14, 23, 27
Write numbers and draw paths to show a sequence of events, and tell a story that involves an interaction of events.	46

If/Then

Objectives	Lessons
Respond to an if-then rule based on illustrations.	6–9
Respond to an if-then rule involving two conditions **(and).**	11–14, 22
Respond to an if-then rule involving one of two possible conditions **(or).**	15, 16, 23
Respond to if-then rules involving **and** and **or.**	17, 18, 21, 26
Construct and apply an if-then rule based on pictures of a familiar character.	29, 31–33, 61
Construct and apply two related if-then rules based on pictures of a familiar character.	34–36, 42, 47
Construct and apply an if-then rule based on dimensions of objects.	49, 51, 52
Apply an if-then rule based on dimensions of objects.	53, 55, 56
Construct displays consistent with different if-then rules.	57, 58, 59
Apply an if-then rule based on the occurrence of events.	63

All, Some, None	Objectives	Lessons
	Follow rules that apply to more than one example (for example: The box next to **every** 4 should have a check mark in it).	**7–9**
	Follow directions involving **all, some** and **none**.	**11–13**

Classification

GROUPS	Identify objects in the class of vehicles.	**11**
	Follow coloring rules for identifying sub-classes of vehicles.	**12, 13**
	Follow coloring rules for identifying objects that belong in a class.	**14**
	Follow rules for identifying objects in more than one class.	**15**
	Follow rules for identifying objects in a class and in a sub-class.	**16, 17**
	Fix up a picture so that specified details are the same.	**15–17, 19**
	Fix up two pictures to follow rules involving classes and sub-classes.	**18, 19, 22**
	Fix up objects in different classes to follow rules for the classes.	**27, 31, 37, 54**
	Identify the class for specified objects and name other members of the same class.	**23, 24, 28**
	Identify objects in a class and apply two rules to a group of objects.	**29, 36, 45**
	Respond to descriptions that distinguish members of a class.	**38, 39, 41**
BINARY LOGIC	Apply a causal rule to specified instances.	**54**
	Respond to story questions involving a causal rule.	**55**
	Apply a binary change rule involving rungs of a ladder.	**56–59**
	Apply a binary change rule to a teeter-totter.	**61–64**

Objectives	Lessons
Follow directions involving **right.** Identify objects that are to the **right** of other objects.	18, 19, 21–24 24
Follow directions involving **right** and **left.**	25–27
Identify objects that are to the **right** and **left** of illustrated elements.	28, 29, 31, 33–35
Orient objects facing different directions and indicate **right** and **left.**	38, 39, 42, 43
Follow and give directions involving **right** and **left** to move an object in a maze.	45, 46
Use directions about **right** and **left** to solve a maze puzzle.	48, 67
Apply **left** and **right** to a rotating object.	49

Questions and Clues

USING

Objectives	Lessons
Use clues to eliminate members of a familiar class.	25, 26, 31, 32
Use clues to figure out the location of specified objects.	27
Use clues to eliminate members of a group of objects.	33, 35
Determine which clue eliminates specific members of a class.	44, 46
Use a glossary and clues to identify the "mystery" objects.	62, 63, 64
Distinguish between good and bad clues for identifying a story character.	69
Use clues to identify objects referred to in familiar stories, and identify the character described in each clue.	70

	Objectives	Lessons
GENERATING	Ask more than one question to figure out the "mystery" picture.	37–39, 41
	Cooperatively develop three questions to identify the "mystery" picture.	43, 44, 47, 48, 56, 57
	Cooperatively develop two clues that identify the "mystery" picture.	49, 51, 53
	Cooperatively use a glossary and develop clues for a specified object.	67, 68

Data

Objectives	Lessons
Collect data on groups and tell whether statements about groups are true or false.	42, 44
Collect and summarize data on right turns and left turns.	51

Alternative Solutions

Objectives	Lessons
Select logical alternatives for fixing up a picture to make an **all** or a **some** statement true.	41, 42
Eliminate members of a set to make **all** statements or **none** statements true.	46, 47
Eliminate members of a set and draw elements to make **all** statements or **none** statements true.	48, 49
Select logical alternatives for fixing up a picture to make a **some** or a **none** statement true.	52, 53

Story Grammar

	Objectives	Lessons
MODEL STORIES	Answer questions about a new story.	1–3, 12, 21, 28, 33, 38, 43–45, 54, 58, 64
	Answer questions about a familiar story.	4–9, 15, 17, 22, 25, 26, 31, 34, 41, 47, 56
	Retell a familiar story.	36, 37, 42, 48
	Answer oral and written questions about a story.	49
	Answer questions about a partially new story.	59, 65
	Listen to a familiar story.	52, 61, 66

	Objectives	Lessons
APPLICATION	Make a picture consistent with the details of the story.	1–6, 9, 11, 12, 15, 17, 21, 22, 25, 26, 28, 31, 33, 34, 38, 41, 43–45, 49, 52, 54, 56
	Fix up a picture according to multiple criteria.	67
EXTRAPOLATION	Relate a familiar story grammar to a picture that indicates the sequence of events for a new story.	11, 16–19, 26, 29, 32, 34, 35, 39, 65
	Identify behaviors of a familiar character.	17
	Identify familiar story characters from unique utterances.	45, 48, 51
	Cooperatively develop utterances for familiar story characters.	52, 66
	Make up an ending to a story based on familiar story grammar.	55, 62, 63
PLAYS	Put on a play to show a new story.	39, 55, 65
	Put on a play to show a familiar story.	40, 57, 60, 61, 67

Writing

Objectives	Lessons
Construct word-picture sentences for different illustrations.	53, 54, 55
Construct sentences for different illustrations.	58, 59, 61, 64, 65, 68
Complete a picture to show a familiar character saying days of the week.	58, 59
Complete a picture and write the days of the week.	61
Complete and construct sentences that describe an action involving **left** and **right**.	62, 63, 66
Complete a picture to show a familiar character saying months of the year.	64, 65, 66
Cooperatively write an ending to a story.	68, 69
Construct three sentences about story characters.	69
Cooperatively write stories about three familiar characters.	70

Skills Profile—Page 1

Student's
name _____

Grade or
year in _____
school

Teacher's name _____

Starting
lesson _____   Date _____

Last lesson   Number of
completed _____   Date _____   days absent _____

Summary of In-program Test Performance

	super star	pretty good worker	have to work harder
Test 1	0–1	2–3	4 or more total errors
Test 2	0–1	2–3	4 or more total errors
Test 3	0–1	2–3	4 or more total errors
Test 4	0–1	2–3	4 or more total errors
Test 5	0–1	2–3	4 or more total errors
Test 6	0–1	2–3	4 or more total errors
Test 7	0–1	2–3	4 or more total errors

Pages 87 to 91 may be reproduced to make a skills profile for each student. These pages show the skills presented in *Reasoning and Writing A* and provide space for indicating the date on which the student completes the lessons in which the skills are taught.

Skills Profile—Page 2   Name _____

Skills	Taught in these Lessons	Date Lessons Completed	Skills	Taught in these Lessons	Date Lessons Completed
FOLLOWING DIRECTIONS			Fixes up pictures to show true statements involving **some**	21–24	
Follows directions involving plural words and singular words	1–2		Fixes up a picture to show true statements involving **all** and **some**	25–45	
Follows directions for marking specified symbols with check marks	1–2		Constructs true statements about a picture that has been changed	28–51	
Follows directions involving position words and plurals	3–4		Fixes up a picture to show false statements involving **all** and **some**	37-39	
Follows directions for marking symbols with specified colors	3–4		**SEQUENCING**		
Follows directions involving position words and the word **not**	5		Performs a sequence of actions based on a series of pictures	1–4	
Follows directions for marking symbols	5–6		Numbers pictures to correspond to a demonstrated series of actions	5–11	
Follows directions involving the words **and** and **not**	6–9		Relates a sequence of actions to a picture with numbers (1, 2, 3, 4) showing where the various actions occurred	7–8	
Follows directions involving **or**	13–14		Relates a familiar story to a picture that has numbers showing where the various events occurred	9–24	
Follows directions involving **same**	14				
Follows directions involving **right** and **left**	25–38		Writes numbers to show a sequence of events and tells a story based on familiar story grammar	13–27	
TRUE/FALSE					
Circles pictures to indicate which actions an animal can do or can't do	1		Writes numbers and draws paths to show a sequence of events and tells a story that involves an interaction of events	46	
Circles the word **true** or **false** for pictures to indicate which actions an animal or person can do or can't do	2–11		**IF-THEN**		
Circles the word **true** or **false** for statements	12–13		Responds to an if-then rule based on illustrations	6–9	
Identifies the pictures for true statements involving **all, some** and **none**	14		Responds to an if-then rule involving two conditions (**and**)	11–22	
Says true statements and false statements for pictures showing **all, some** and **none**	15–16		Responds to an if-then rule involving one of two possible conditions (**or**)	15–23	
Fixes up pictures to show true statements involving **all**	18–19		Responds to if-then rules involving **and** and **or**	17–26	

Skills Profile—Page 3　Name_____

Skills	Taught in these Lessons	Date Lessons Completed	Skills	Taught in these Lessons	Date Lessons Completed
Constructs and applies an if-then rule based on pictures of a familiar character	29–61		Fixes up two pictures to follow rules involving classes and sub-classes	18–22	
Constructs and applies two related if-then rules based on pictures of a familiar character	34–47		Fixes up objects in different classes to follow rules for the classes	27–54	
Constructs and applies an if-then rule based on dimensions of objects	49–52		For specified objects, identifies the class and other members of the same class	23–28	
Applies an if-then rule based on dimensions of objects	53–56		Identifies objects in a class and applies two rules to a group of objects	29–45	
Constructs displays consistent with different if-then rules	57–59		Responds to descriptions that distinguish members of a class	38–41	
Applies an if-then rule based on the occurrence of events	63		**Binary Logic**		
ALL, SOME, NONE			Applies a causal rule to specified instances	54	
Follows rules that apply to more than one example	7–9		Responds to story questions involving a causal rule	55	
Follows directions involving **all, some** and **none**	11–13		Applies a binary change rule involving rungs of a ladder	56–59	
CLASSIFICATION			Applies a binary change rule to a teeter-totter	61–64	
Groups			**RIGHT/LEFT**		
Identifies objects in the class of vehicles	11		Follows directions involving **right**	18–24	
Follows coloring rules for identifying sub-classes of vehicles	12–13		Identifies objects that are to the **right** of other objects	24	
Follows coloring rules for identifying objects that belong in a class	14		Follows directions involving **right** and **left**	25–27	
Follows rules for identifying objects in more than one class	15		Identifies objects that are to the **right** and **left** of illustrated elements	28–35	
Follows rules for identifying objects in a class and in a sub-class	16–17		Orients objects facing different directions and indicates **right** and **left**	38–43	
Fixes up a picture so that specified details are the same	15–19		Follows and gives directions involving **right** and **left** to move an object in a maze	45–46	

Skills Profile—Page 4 Name_____

Skills	Taught in these Lessons	Date Lessons Completed	Skills	Taught in these Lessons	Date Lessons Completed
Uses directions about **right** and **left** to solve a maze puzzle	48–67		**DATA**		
Applies **right** and **left** to a rotating object	49		Collects data on groups and tells whether statements about groups are true or false	42–44	
QUESTIONS AND CLUES			Collects and summarizes data on right turns and left turns	51	
Using			**ALTERNATIVE SOLUTIONS**		
Uses clues to eliminate members of a familiar class	25–32		Selects logical alternatives for fixing up a picture to make an **all** or a **some** statement true	41–42	
Uses clues to figure out the location of specified objects	27				
Uses clues to eliminate members of a group of objects	33–35		Eliminates members of a set to make **all** statements or **none** statements true	46–47	
Determines which clue eliminates specific members of a class	44–46		Eliminates members of a set and draws elements to make **all** statements or **none** statements true	48–49	
Uses a glossary and clues to identify the "mystery" objects	62–64				
Distinguishes between good and bad clues for identifying a story character	69		Selects logical alternatives for fixing up a picture to make a **some** or a **none** statement true	52–53	
Uses clues to identify objects referred to in familiar stories, and identifies the character described in each clue	70		**STORY GRAMMAR**		
			Model Stories		
			Answers questions about a new story	1–64	
Generating			Answers questions about a familiar story	4–56	
Asks more than one question to figure out the "mystery" picture	37–41		Retells a familiar story	36–48	
Retells a familiar story	36–48		Answers oral and written questions about a story	49	
Cooperatively develops three questions to identify the "mystery" picture	43–57		Answers questions about a partially new story	59, 65	
			Listens to a familiar story	52, 61–66	
Cooperatively develops two clues that identify the "mystery" picture	49–53		**Application**		
			Makes a picture consistent with the details of a story	1–56	
Cooperatively uses a glossary and develops clues for a specified object	67–68		Fixes up a picture according to multiple criteria	67	
			Extrapolation		
			Relates a familiar story grammar to a picture that indicates the sequence of events for a new story	11–65	

Skills Profile—Page 5 Name _____

Skills	Taught in these Lessons	Date Lessons Completed	Skills	Taught in these Lessons	Date Lessons Completed
Identifies behaviors of a familiar character	17		**WRITING**		
Identifies familiar story characters from unique utterances	45–51		Constructs word-picture sentences for different illustrations	53–55	
Cooperatively develops utterances for familiar story characters	52–66		Constructs sentences for different illustrations	58–68	
Makes up an ending to a story based on familiar story grammar	55–63		Completes a picture to show a familiar character saying days of the week	58–59	
Plays			Completes a picture and writes the days of the week	61	
Puts on a play to show a new story	39–65		Completes and constructs sentences that describe an action involving right and left	62–66	
Puts on a play to show a familiar story	40–67		Completes a picture to show a familiar character saying months of the year	64–66	
			Cooperatively writes an ending to a story	68–69	
			Constructs three sentences about story characters	69	
			Cooperatively writes stories about three familiar characters	70	

Reproducible Group Summary Sheet—Summary of Errors

Names	Test 1 Total				Test 2 Total					Test 3 Total				Test 4 Total			Test 5 Total			Test 6 Total			Objects (blanks)	Numbers (boxes)	Test 7 Total
	A	B	C		A	B	C	D		A	B	C		A	B	C		A	B		A	B	C			